1-50

MARSHALL MINI

WEATHER

A Marshall Edition
Conceived, edited and designed by
Marshall Editions Ltd
The Orangery
161 New Bond Street
London W1S 2UF

First published in the UK in 2001 by
Marshall Publishing Ltd

10 9 8 7 6 5 4 3 2 1

ISBN 1 84028 392 0

Originated in Singapore by Master Image
Printed in Hong Kong by Imago

Consultant: Don Hewitt (The Met Office College)
Designers: Nelupa Hussain, Caroline Sangster
Managing Designer: Siân Williams
Design Assistant: Ella Butler
Art Director: Simon Webb
Managing Editor: Claire Sipi
Editorial Manager: Kate Phelps
Publishing Director: Linda Cole
Proofreader: Lindsay McTeague
Production: Nikki Ingram, Anna Pauletti
Picture Researcher: Antonella Mauro

MARSHALL MINI
WEATHER

Sue Nicholson

MARSHALL PUBLISHING • LONDON

Contents

. . . .

Weather systems

The ever-changing skies reflect the vast movements in the atmosphere, where most of the Earth's weather systems form.

What is the weather?

Weather is what is happening outside in the air, now. It is all the day to day changes in temperature, wind, rain and sunshine in any place on the Earth.

Rain or shine?

What's the weather like today? It may be sunny and hot, or rainy and cold. In some parts of the world, the weather stays the same for long periods of time. In other places, it changes from day to day. Sometimes weather can be dangerous. Storms, floods and droughts can cause many deaths, so it is vital for us to study and try to forecast the weather. The study of the weather is called meteorology, and the scientists who study it are called meteorologists.

The weather affects us all. It may determine what kind of clothes we wear, whether we need to put on sunscreen lotion, or whether we should carry umbrellas.

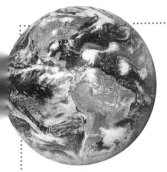

In this satellite image clouds whirl across the Earth.

The world's weather

All over the world, at this very moment, people are experiencing different kinds of weather. In some places it will be calm and sunny with clear blue skies. In others, there will be light rain, or drizzle. In still others, there may be hurricane-force winds or torrential rain and lightning strikes.

Layers of air

The Earth is surrounded by a warm blanket of air, called the atmosphere, which protects the Earth from the fierce heat and harmful rays of the Sun. The atmosphere is made up of several layers. Nearly all of our weather forms in the troposphere – the layer of air closest to the Earth's surface.

Satellite images from space show weather forecasters where storms are developing.

Height
960 km
(600 miles)

Exosphere

Aurora
(shimmering lights caused by bursts of energy from the Sun)

480 km
(300 miles)

Thermosphere

Sprite

80 km
(50 miles)

Mesosphere

Stratosphere

Troposphere

50 km
(30 miles)

Thunderstorms
(see pages 40–43)

Frontal depression
(see pages 26–27)

15 km
(10 miles)

High cirrus clouds along jet stream
(see pages 28–29)

Occluding frontal depression
(see pages 26–27)

Hurricane
(see pages 50–53)

The weather machine

The weather is like a giant machine, driven by energy (or "fuel") from the Sun. The interaction of the Sun, air and water is very complex. Together, these elements make and affect our weather.

Sun power

The Sun heats and drives the Earth's atmosphere, moving air and water around the globe. However, the Sun does not heat the Earth's atmosphere evenly. This is because its rays hit the Earth at different angles in different places. The Sun's heat is most intense at the equator, where its rays hit the Earth's surface directly, and less intense at the poles.

Sun's rays

Reflecting the Sun's energy

Some parts of the Earth's surface reflect the Sun's heat, affecting the temperature in a particular place. Snow and ice reflect 90 per cent of the Sun's heat. Asphalt roads reflect only 5 per cent and absorb the rest.

Sun's rays

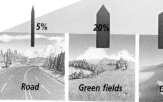

5% **Road**

20% **Green fields**

45% **Desert**

90% **Snow and ice**

Wind power

Warm moist air moves around the Earth as winds, from hot places to cold places. This movement of air helps to even out the unequal distribution of heat over the Earth's surface. But because the Earth spins on its axis, the winds may be bent off course. Winds may also be disrupted by huge storms or blocked by tall mountain ranges.

Gale-force winds whip up waves at sea.

Water power

The water in Earth's atmosphere is continually moving in an endless cycle called the water cycle. Water from rivers, lakes, oceans, plants and animals evaporates and enters the atmosphere as water vapour (1). As the air rises, it cools, and the water vapour condenses to form clouds (2). Clouds return water to the Earth's surface as precipitation – rain, hail or snow (3). The water then runs off the land into the ground (4) and returns to the rivers and oceans.

The water cycle

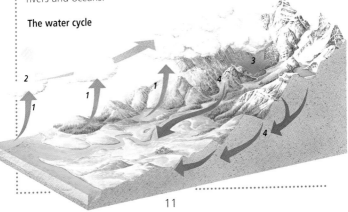

How clouds form

The air is always moist because it contains water vapour. We only see the water vapour when it condenses into tiny droplets, which remain suspended in the air as clouds.

Making clouds

Clouds form in the troposphere – the layer of air nearest Earth in which most of our weather occurs. In this part of the atmosphere, temperature decreases with height and in the upper part of the troposphere it is well below freezing, at about –55°C (–67°F). Most clouds form when air rising in the troposphere is cooled until the water vapour condenses into liquid. When it is very cold, the water vapour freezes straight into ice crystals. On a sunny day, areas of bare soil or rock heat up more than the surrounding land. The land heats the air above it and the air rises in a bubble, called a thermal. The air condenses and a small cloud forms. The wind carries the cloud away and more clouds are formed in the same way.

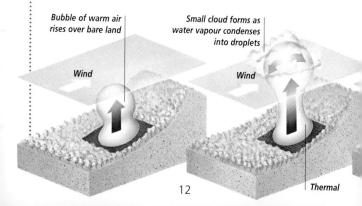

Bubble of warm air rises over bare land

Small cloud forms as water vapour condenses into droplets

Wind

Wind

Thermal

Fog often forms in valley bottoms on calm, clear nights.

Low cloud

Fog, or mist, is simply cloud lying close to the ground. It often forms on clear nights, when the rapidly cooling ground cools the air just above it and the water vapour condenses into droplets. This kind of fog is usually burned off by the Sun's heat the following morning. (See page 109 for some facts on types of fog.)

When clouds form

Clouds form in four main ways: when the Sun warms the ground, creating thermals or rising air (1); when air rises over a mountain (2); when air from opposite directions meets and is forced upwards (3); and when a mass of cold air flows under warm, lighter air (4).

1 Over warm ground

2 Over hills and mountains

3 Air meets and rises

4 Cold air mass pushes up warmer, lighter air

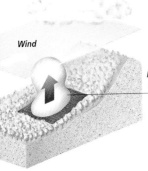

Cloud drifts away and a new cloud begins to form on the bubble of rising air

Wind

New bubble of air forms

13

Types of clouds

Clouds can be different sizes, shapes and thicknesses according to the forces that caused the air to rise, cool and make them.

Cloud	Altitude	
Cirrostratus	13 km	8 miles
Cumulonimbus	11 km	7 miles
Cirrus		
HIGH CLOUDS	10 km	6 miles
Cirrocumulus	8 km	5 miles
Altocumulus	6 km	4 miles
MEDIUM-LEVEL CLOUDS		
Altostratus	5 km	3 miles
Stratocumulus	3 km	2 miles
Cumulus LOW CLOUDS	1.6 km	1 mile
Stratus		
Nimbostratus	Sea level	

Cloud names

Clouds were first classified by Luke Howard (1772–1864), who used Latin words to describe them. Cumulus means a heap, or pile; stratus means a layer; cirrus means a tuft or filament (for example, of hair); and nimbus means bearing rain. There are 10 main cloud types, with names based on combinations of these words.

Cumulus

Fluffy cumulus clouds often form on a sunny day when air rises over a sun-warmed slope or field. Altocumulus are medium-level clouds. (*Alto* is Latin for high but is used today for medium-level clouds.) If a cumulus continues to grow it may form a massive cumulonimbus, or thunderhead cloud, thousands of metres (feet) deep.

Stratus

Stratus clouds, or layer clouds, are often formed when a mass of warm air slowly rises and spreads over a mass of cold air or over a mountain. Altostratus clouds (like altocumulus clouds) may be made up of both water droplets and ice crystals. Nimbostratus clouds are usually grey in colour and indicate that it will rain.

Cirrus

Cirrus clouds usually appear as wispy white strands or as white patches or bands. Along with cirrocumulus (about 8 km/ 5 miles) and cirrostratus (about 13 km/8 miles), they form high in the troposphere, at about 11 km (7 miles) or more, and are made up of ice crystals.

Rain

It only rains when millions of tiny cloud droplets in clouds join together to form larger water droplets that are big and heavy enough to fall to the ground.

The type of precipitation depends on whether a cloud carries water droplets, ice crystals, or both. Low-level shallow clouds contain only water droplets, so they produce drizzle or rain. Deeper clouds contain both water droplets and ice crystals, so they may produce rain, snow or sleet.

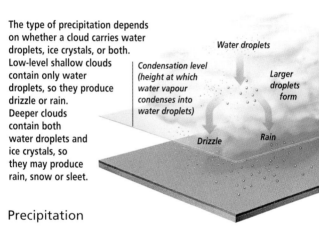

Water droplets

Condensation level (height at which water vapour condenses into water droplets)

Larger droplets form

Drizzle *Rain*

Precipitation

All the different kinds of moisture that come from the atmosphere are called precipitation. Precipitation includes rain, snow, drizzle, sleet and hail. The air inside a cloud is constantly moving. As it moves, tiny water droplets bump into each other, forming larger droplets. Eventually, the droplets become too big to stay suspended in the cloud and fall to the ground. Raindrops can grow to 5 mm (¼ in) wide. Because larger droplets fall faster than smaller ones, the start of a shower of rain is often marked by a heavier burst of rainfall. In order for snow to fall, a large number of ice crystals must be stuck together to form individual snowflakes that are large and heavy enough to reach the ground.

Sometimes, water droplets freeze on to ice crystals, making a clear ice pellet or a milky snow pellet. The Americans call this sleet. To the British, sleet is snow that is melting as it falls, or a mixture of snow and rain. Hail forms in cumulonimbus clouds (see pages 18–19).

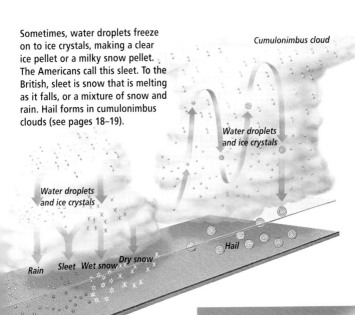

Cumulonimbus cloud

Water droplets and ice crystals

Water droplets and ice crystals

Rain *Sleet* *Wet snow* *Dry snow* *Hail*

Rainbows

When sunlight shines through millions of water droplets, a rainbow forms. Each droplet acts like a tiny prism, splitting the light into the seven colours of the spectrum – red, orange, yellow, green, blue, indigo and violet (see page 75 for diagram). A rainbow's colours are usually brightest and clearest at either end, or foot, where the largest raindrops occur.

A rainbow is a natural spectrum – its colours are the colours of sunlight.

17

Hail and snow

Snow is precipitation from clouds in the form of ice crystals. Hail is frozen ice pellets that form inside cumulonimbus clouds. Hailstones are usually pea-sized, but can grow dangerously large.

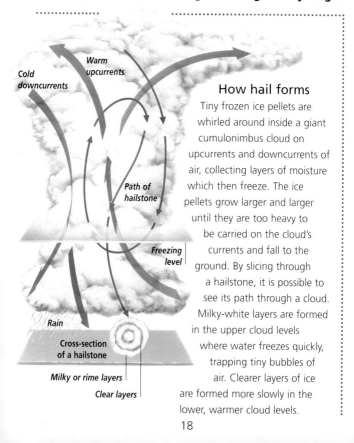

Cold downcurrents

Warm upcurrents

Path of hailstone

Freezing level

Rain

Cross-section of a hailstone

Milky or rime layers

Clear layers

How hail forms

Tiny frozen ice pellets are whirled around inside a giant cumulonimbus cloud on upcurrents and downcurrents of air, collecting layers of moisture which then freeze. The ice pellets grow larger and larger until they are too heavy to be carried on the cloud's currents and fall to the ground. By slicing through a hailstone, it is possible to see its path through a cloud. Milky-white layers are formed in the upper cloud levels where water freezes quickly, trapping tiny bubbles of air. Clearer layers of ice are formed more slowly in the lower, warmer cloud levels.

Snowflakes

Tiny ice crystals join together to form beautiful hexagonal (six-sided) star shapes, or snowflakes. Most snowflakes melt before they reach the ground. They only fall as snow when the air near the ground is cold enough. Because snowflakes are so delicate, they often break up as they fall, but may clump together with other flakes. No two snowflakes are alike – each is unique like a fingerprint. "Dry" snow falls when it is very cold and the ice crystals do not stick together easily. Dry snow is fine and powdery. "Wet" snow falls at temperatures near freezing point, and the snowflakes tend to be larger because the ice crystals stick together more easily.

Frost

On clear, calm nights, the air may be cooled so much that some of its water vapour condenses to form a thin layer of water called dew. On colder nights, when the temperature falls below freezing point, this water vapour freezes into ice crystals, forming a hoar frost. This covers the ground with gleaming white needlelike crystals. Rime looks similar to hoar frost but is thicker. It often forms in fog.

A spring frost may damage or even kill young plants.

Breezes and winds

Air moves around the Earth's surface as wind. Winds can blow on a small local scale or on a much larger global scale.

Air pressure

Winds blow because of changes in air pressure. Air pressure is the force, or weight, of air pressing down on the ground. When air warms, its particles expand, become less dense and rise. Because there is less air pushing down on the ground, an area of low air pressure, called a depression or a low, is created. When air cools, its particles move closer together, or become more dense, and sink. As cool air presses down on the ground, it creates an area of high pressure, called an anticyclone or a high.

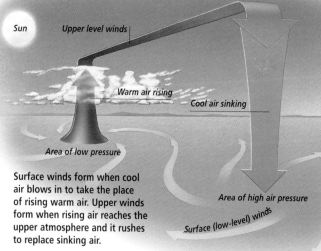

Sun

Upper level winds

Warm air rising

Cool air sinking

Area of low pressure

Area of high air pressure

Surface (low-level) winds

Surface winds form when cool air blows in to take the place of rising warm air. Upper winds form when rising air reaches the upper atmosphere and it rushes to replace sinking air.

Local coastal breezes

In places by the sea, the wind changes direction during the day and at night. By day, the land heats up faster than the sea, warming the air above it, which then rises. Cool air blows inland from the sea to take the place of the rising warmer air. At night, the land cools faster than the sea so the wind changes direction and blows from the land out to sea.

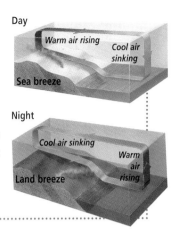

Day

Warm air rising

Cool air sinking

Sea breeze

Night

Cool air sinking

Warm air rising

Land breeze

A paraglider floats on bubbles of rising warm air.

When winds blow

Winds blow when cool air moves in to take the place of warm air or, in other words, when air moves from an area of high pressure to an area of low pressure. The greater the difference in air pressure between highs and lows, the stronger the force of the wind.

Highs and lows

Highs usually bring good, sunny weather with light breezes or winds. Lows usually mean bad weather, with heavy clouds and strong winds. Winds do not always blow evenly. Gusty winds often form over bumpy ground and can veer, or change direction, quite suddenly.

Weather patterns

The Sun's uneven heating of the
Earth's surface greatly affects
the world's climate.

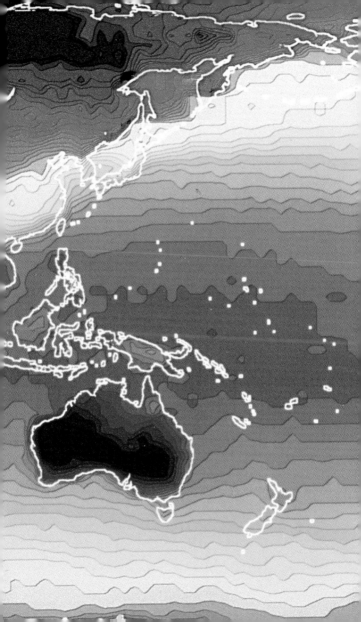

The world's winds

Large areas of rising air, which produce clouds and storms, and large areas of sinking air, which produce drier weather, create a pattern of winds around the Earth known as the global circulation.

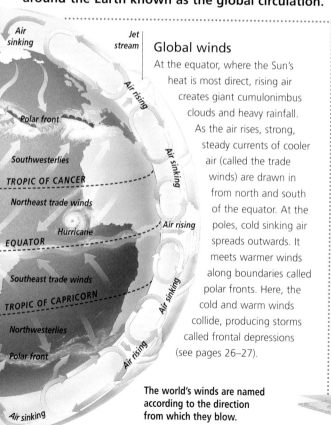

Air sinking

Jet stream

Air rising

Polar front

Southwesterlies

TROPIC OF CANCER

Northeast trade winds

Air sinking

Hurricane

Air rising

EQUATOR

Southeast trade winds

TROPIC OF CAPRICORN

Air sinking

Northwesterlies

Polar front

Air rising

Air sinking

Global winds

At the equator, where the Sun's heat is most direct, rising air creates giant cumulonimbus clouds and heavy rainfall. As the air rises, strong, steady currents of cooler air (called the trade winds) are drawn in from north and south of the equator. At the poles, cold sinking air spreads outwards. It meets warmer winds along boundaries called polar fronts. Here, the cold and warm winds collide, producing storms called frontal depressions (see pages 26–27).

The world's winds are named according to the direction from which they blow.

24

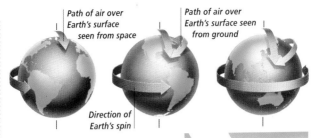

Path of air over Earth's surface seen from space

Path of air over Earth's surface seen from ground

Direction of Earth's spin

Coriolis force

The world's winds do not blow in straight lines because the Earth is constantly spinning west to east. For example, as a wind blows south, the places over which it passes move east, so the path of the wind curves.

When seen from the ground, the wind's path curves. This is due to the Coriolis force.

Mountain winds

As a wind moves over high mountains, it loses its water vapour in the form of clouds, rain or snow. It then blows from an area of low air pressure on the mountain top to an area of low air pressure in the valley bottom. This movement compresses the air (squeezes it into a smaller space) and warms it. A dry, hot wind blowing from mountains is called the Santa Ana in southern California, a chinook in the Rockies, and a föhn in the European Alps.

Air loses moisture and becomes drier and warmer as it passes over high mountains.

Air rises, forming clouds and precipitation

Warm dry air

Cool air carrying water vapour

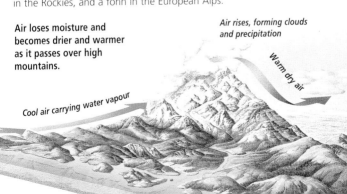

Weather fronts

A weather front is the name given to the boundary where two air masses meet. Fronts result in changeable weather, often bringing clouds and rain.

Warm and cold fronts

Unsettled weather often arises in the mid-latitudes (the area halfway between the equator and the poles), where warm tropical air masses meet cold polar air masses. A bulge of warm air pushes into the cold air, and the air begins to rotate around a centre of low pressure, or a depression. At the warm front, the warm air rises over the cold air, producing clouds and light rain. At the cold front, cold air pushes in, behind and under the warm air, producing heavier clouds and rain. This "frontal depression" may last several days.

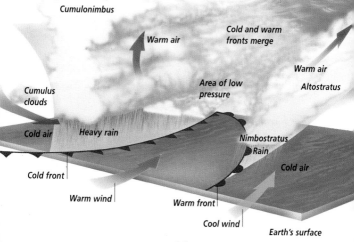

Cumulonimbus

Warm air

Cold and warm fronts merge

Warm air

Cumulus clouds

Area of low pressure

Altostratus

Cold air

Heavy rain

Nimbostratus
Rain

Cold air

Cold front

Warm wind

Warm front

Cool wind

Earth's surface

As a cold front passes, cumulonimbus clouds break up, showing patches of clearer sky.

Occluded fronts

An occluded front occurs when a cold front catches up with a warm front and cuts it off from the ground so that the cold front lies between two masses of cold air. The frontal depression then dissolves, or occludes. A warm occlusion occurs if the cold front rises over the warm front. A cold occlusion occurs if the cold front cuts underneath the warm front.

Cirrus

Cirrostratus

As a warm front approaches, cirrus clouds give way to cirrostratus, then altostratus and nimbostratus clouds. A cold front brings cumulonimbus and heavy rain.

Moving fronts

A frontal depression in its most developed stage may be a large storm up to 1,600 km (1,000 miles) wide and may travel thousands of kilometres (miles), bringing stormy and changeable weather to many regions before it finally

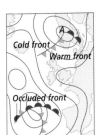

Cold front

Warm front

Occluded front

dissolves. Moving fronts are plotted on weather maps as curved lines (see also pages 72–73).

On weather maps, a frontal depression appears as a kink (A).

Jet streams

Weather fronts near the Earth's surface are driven by jet streams – fast-flowing rivers of air that form a high-level boundary in the Earth's atmosphere between polar and tropical air masses.

Rivers of air

Jet streams are fast-flowing rivers of air around 480 km (300 miles) wide and 6 km (4 miles) deep that circle the Earth from west to east 10 km (6 miles) above the ground. There are jet streams in both the northern and southern hemispheres. Sometimes they flow in straight lines, but often they zigzag. When a jet stream loops away from the north or south pole, it makes a shape like a trough. Most frontal depressions tend to form below a trough made by a jet stream along one of the polar fronts.

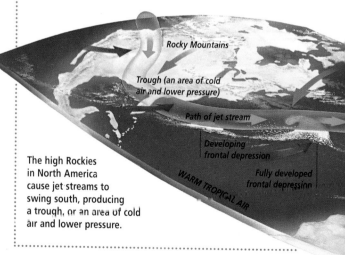

Rocky Mountains

Trough (an area of cold air and lower pressure)

Path of jet stream

Developing frontal depression

Fully developed frontal depression

WARM TROPICAL AIR

The high Rockies in North America cause jet streams to swing south, producing a trough, or an area of cold air and lower pressure.

Jet speed

Jet streams get their energy from the difference in temperature between the cold and warm air across a polar front. The greater the temperature difference, the faster the jet stream. Jet streams can blow at speeds of around 300–600 km/h (200–400 mph). Aircraft travelling east across the globe take advantage of powerful jet streams to speed up travelling time.

Eastbound aircraft take one hour less to fly across North America than those travelling west into the face of a jet stream.

Looping path

If weather forecasters know the position of a jet stream, they can work out which places will be affected by changeable and stormy weather in the depression below the jet stream. However, jet streams change position each day and their paths are hard to plot.

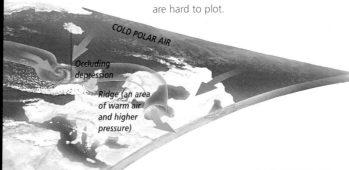

COLD POLAR AIR

Occluding depression

Ridge (an area of warm air and higher pressure)

Winds and the ocean

The oceans carry warm water from the tropics to the poles, helping to balance global heat and making the oceans an important part of the world's weather machine.

Surface ocean currents

Because surface ocean currents are created by global winds, they move in the same direction as the winds. They move in two clockwise circulations in the northern hemisphere (in the north Atlantic and north Pacific oceans) and three anticlockwise circulations in the southern hemisphere (in the south Atlantic, south Pacific and Indian oceans). These circulations are called gyres.

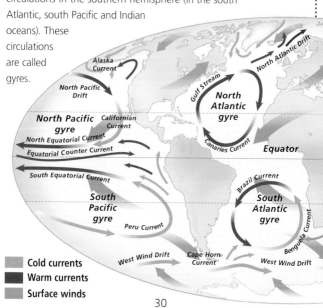

Alaska Current

North Pacific Drift

Gulf Stream

North Atlantic Drift

North Atlantic gyre

North Pacific gyre Californian Current

North Equatorial Current

Equatorial Counter Current

Canaries Current

Equator

South Equatorial Current

Brazil Current

South Pacific gyre

Peru Current

South Atlantic gyre

Benguela Current

West Wind Drift

Cape Horn Current

West Wind Drift

Cold currents
Warm currents
Surface winds

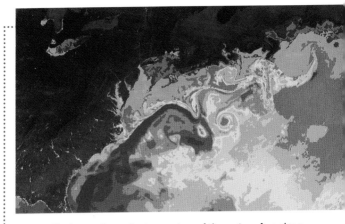

This satellite image shows the temperature of the sea's surface along the coast of North America. The Gulf Stream is shown in red.

The Gulf Stream

Warm water from the Gulf of Mexico is carried along the Florida coast by the ocean currrent known as the Gulf Stream. It continues across the North Atlantic as the North Atlantic Drift, warming the shores of the United Kingdom, Norway and Iceland.

Kuro Shio

North Pacific gyre

North Equatorial Current

Equatorial Counter Current

Monsoon Drift

North Equatorial Current

South Indian gyre

East Australian Current

South Equatorial Current

West Australian Current

West Wind Drift

Deep ocean currents

Currents also flow deep in the world's ocean, from the cold poles towards the warmer equator. Deep ocean currents are much more slow-moving than surface currents. Some deep ocean currents take thousands of years to reach the surface.

Weather and climate

Climate is the usual pattern of weather in a place over a long period of time. In some areas, this pattern changes throughout the year. In others, it remains the same.

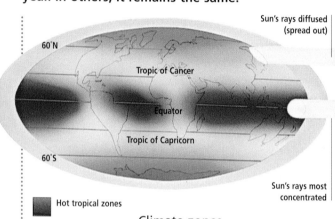

Sun's rays diffused (spread out)

60°N

Tropic of Cancer

Equator

Tropic of Capricorn

60°S

Sun's rays most concentrated

Hot tropical zones

Temperate zones

Cold polar zones

Climate zones

An area's climate depends mainly on its latitude – how far north or south of the equator it is. The world has three main climate zones. Cold polar zones are found around the poles; hotter tropical zones are found on and around the equator; and warm temperate zones are found between the poles and the tropics. The world's climate can be divided still further (see page 34). Climate is also affected by altitude (how far a place is above sea level). Usually, the higher the land, the cooler the temperature. Coastal climates are affected by whether there is a warm or cold ocean current flowing nearby.

Desert climates

In desert areas, there is no plant life to reflect the Sun's heat. Most of the heat is therefore absorbed and the desert becomes extremely hot. At night, heat is lost rapidly from the land and the desert becomes bitterly cold.

Desert climates remain the same all year.

City climates

Roads and buildings in a city absorb a lot of heat from the Sun. Heat is also released from homes, factories and cars. This makes cities much warmer than the surrounding countryside. Rising warm air over cities also increases cloud depths, usually resulting in more rainfall.

Cities may be 10°C (18°F) warmer than the surrounding countryside.

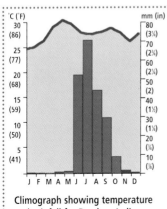

Climograph showing temperature and rainfall for Bombay, India

Climographs

A place's climate is usually defined by its temperature and rainfall. Climatologists, who study climate, often summarise the climate of a region or city on a climograph. This combines the place's average monthly rainfall (shown on a bar chart) and its average monthly temperatures (shown on a graph).

33

Climate zones

The world's different climates affect the kinds of plants that grow and animals that live there. They also help to shape the Earth's land.

World climates

Places around the world can be grouped into climate zones even though they are far apart. Some climatologists disagree about the number and description of climate zones. However, the nine zones given here are generally accepted groups. Some climate zones are named according to the typical vegetation that grows there. This plant life (and the animal life that it supports) has adapted to a particular climate over a long period of time. Climate zones may change over time. For example, millions of years ago, much of the Earth's land was covered in ice (see pages 84–85).

Mediterranean
Mild winter, warm summer

Tropical rainforest
Hot and wet all year

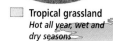

Tropical grassland
Hot all year, wet and dry seasons

Inland climates

The inland areas of large landmasses, such as North America and Asia, have more extreme climates than coastal areas. Places such as Canada and Siberia heat up over the summer but become very cold in the winter and are usually covered by snow and ice.

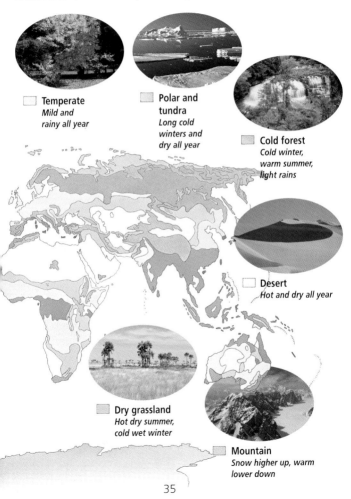

Temperate
Mild and rainy all year

Polar and tundra
Long cold winters and dry all year

Cold forest
Cold winter, warm summer, light rains

Desert
Hot and dry all year

Dry grassland
Hot dry summer, cold wet winter

Mountain
Snow higher up, warm lower down

Weather and the seasons

Seasonal weather changes according to the time of year. Some places have four seasons – spring, summer, autumn and winter. Others have the same sort of weather all year round.

Summer and winter

To understand the seasons, you need to know how the Earth moves through space. The Earth orbits, or travels around, the Sun once a year. At the same time, it is spinning around on its axis (an imaginary line from pole to pole). As it spins, the Earth is tilted at about 23.5 degrees. The tilt of the Earth as it orbits the Sun produces the seasons. When the North Pole is tilted towards the Sun, the northern hemisphere receives more light and warmth and it is summer. When the South Pole is tilted towards the Sun, it is summer in the southern hemisphere.

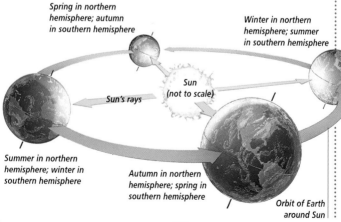

Spring in northern hemisphere; autumn in southern hemisphere

Winter in northern hemisphere; summer in southern hemisphere

Sun (not to scale)

Sun's rays

Summer in northern hemisphere; winter in southern hemisphere

Autumn in northern hemisphere; spring in southern hemisphere

Orbit of Earth around Sun

In temperate climates, in late spring and early summer fresh green leaves appear on trees and other plants.

In the autumn, the leaves change colour to russet reds, yellows and golds before falling off the trees at the onset of winter.

Changing seasons

Generally, the farther north or south a region is from the equator, the more distinct are its seasons. The changing seasons have a great effect on plant and animal life. Some animals hibernate through the long, cold winter months. Others make seasonal migrations in autumn to warmer climates to find plentiful supplies of food, returning the following spring.

Tropical climates

Areas on the equator receive the same amount of sunlight all year round, so they do not have a summer and winter. They have a tropical climate, with fairly even rainfall throughout the year. Regions farther north or south of the equator have wetter seasons, with more rain.

Rainforests grow in hot, wet tropical climates.

37

Extreme weather

Severe weather can bring death and devastation. Hurricane Andrew swept through Florida in August 1992, flattening and flooding homes and ripping trees from the ground.

Thunderstorms

Thunderstorms are best known for thunder and lightning, but they may also bring heavy rain and floods, huge hailstones and sometimes tornadoes.

How a thunderstorm forms

A thunderstorm forms in a small cumulus cloud when warm moist air is heated close to the ground and rises quickly, creating an upcurrent (1). Upcurrents and downcurrents sweep water droplets and ice crystals together until they become electrified. Electrical charges in the cloud slowly build up until a massive spark of lightning is discharged in a flash (2). The thunderstorm only dies down when the upcurrent stops (3).

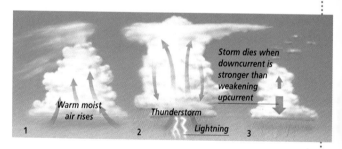

Warm moist air rises

Thunderstorm

Lightning

Storm dies when downcurrent is stronger than weakening upcurrent

1
2
3

Cool air | Very hot air | Very hot air | Cool air

What is thunder?

Thunder is the sound of air expanding very quickly and producing shockwaves as it is heated to around 30,000°C (54,000°F) in the fraction of a second. It rumbles because of the timelag between shockwaves along the path of lightning.

40

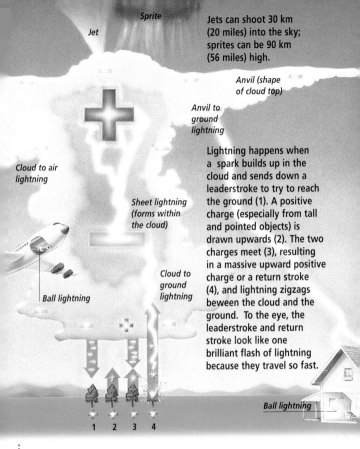

Sprite

Jet

Jets can shoot 30 km (20 miles) into the sky; sprites can be 90 km (56 miles) high.

Anvil (shape of cloud top)

Anvil to ground lightning

Cloud to air lightning

Sheet lightning (forms within the cloud)

Cloud to ground lightning

Ball lightning

Lightning happens when a spark builds up in the cloud and sends down a leaderstroke to try to reach the ground (1). A positive charge (especially from tall and pointed objects) is drawn upwards (2). The two charges meet (3), resulting in a massive upward positive charge or a return stroke (4), and lightning zigzags beween the cloud and the ground. To the eye, the leaderstroke and return stroke look like one brilliant flash of lightning because they travel so fast.

Ball lightning

1   2   3   4

Types of lightning

Lightning can flash to the ground as forked lightning, flash to another cloud, or simply die out and disappear in the air. Sheet lightning happens inside the cloud and is seen as a sudden brightening of the cloud. Ball lightning is rare but may appear suddenly in a room and disappear within seconds through an open window. Narrow blue jets or glowing sprites may appear in the sky high above thunderstorms.

Living with lightning

At any moment, there are nearly 1,800 thunderstorms raging around the world, generating as many as 100 flashes of lightning a minute. In the United States alone, about 100 people get killed by lightning every year.

From flash to rumble

The light from a flash of lightning reaches you almost at once, but the sound of thunder travels more slowly, at 340 m per second (1,130 ft per second). To calculate how far away the centre of a thunderstorm is, count the seconds between seeing the lightning flash and hearing the thunder rumble then divide by three for kilometres (five for miles). If you do this several times, you can work out whether the storm is getting closer.

Lightning travels at about 140,000 km (87,000 miles) per second – almost half the speed of light.

Lightning destroyed this tree.

Lightning damage

Lightning always takes the easiest path to the ground, which is usually through a high point, such as a tree or building. Tall buildings are protected by lightning conductors (strips of copper connecting a metal spike on the roof to a metal plate on the ground) to give the lightning an easy, harmless route to Earth. Trees may be severely damaged or destroyed by lightning. Lightning may also spark forest fires.

Safety first

Here are some do's and don'ts if you are caught in a thunderstorm.
DON'T shelter under a tree or stay out in wide open fields, on a beach or hilltop.
DON'T use golf clubs, umbrellas or fishing rods, which may attract a leaderstroke.
DO shelter indoors (but away from metal sinks, radiators and window frames) or in a hard-topped car.

If far from shelter, crouch down and bend forwards with your hands on your knees (do not lie flat on the ground).

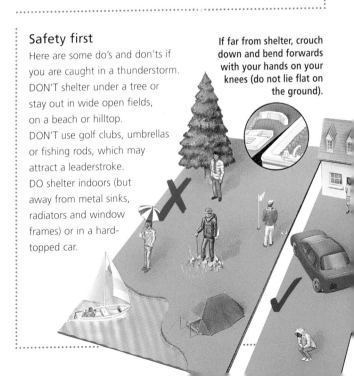

Downbursts and ice falls

**Downbursts are severe local winds blasting
down from a thunderstorm with incredible force.
Macrobursts are larger, microbursts smaller. Strong
thunderstorm upcurrents cause ice falls – or hail.**

Flying in a storm

Aircraft avoid flying through thunderstorms. Within cumulonimbus
clouds, rapidly changing wind directions and wind speeds (called
wind shear) can make the flight bumpy and even damage the
airplane. Downbursts can even slam an airplane to the ground.
To try to overcome these problems, airline pilots are trained using
virtual reality computers so they can cope with the powerful winds
associated with a severe downburst. These winds can reach speeds
of up to 270 km/h (170 mph).

Pilots are usually most wary
of microbursts because they
are harder to detect and avoid
than larger macrobursts. In a
microburst, an aircraft experiences
a headwind and uplift, which
suddenty switches to a tailwind
and downcurrent. The pilot has
only seconds to adjust the
controls before being
slammed to the
ground.

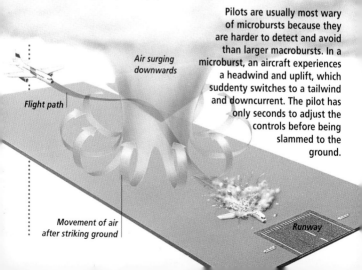

Air surging downwards

Flight path

Movement of air after striking ground

Runway

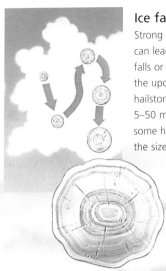

Ice falls

Strong upcurrents in thunderclouds can lead to another danger – ice falls or hailstones. The more powerful the upcurrents, the bigger the hailstones. Most hailstones are 5–50 mm (¼–2 in) wide, but some have been reported to be the size of grapefruits.

Hailstones grow in size, gathering layers of ice, as they are swept up and down inside a cumulonimbus. Most are round but some are chunky and spiky.

Severe damage

Hailstones can cause millions of dollars worth of damage every year to crops grown in the Great Plains region of the United States. There, farmers call the hailstone threat the "white plague". Hailstones can also break windows and street lights, dent cars and planes, batter roofs and cause injuries to people. Severe hailstorms are also common in China, Bangladesh and India, where they kill and injure hundreds of people a year.

Corn crop beaten flat by hailstones.

45

Tornadoes

A tornado, or twister, is a powerful funnel-shaped whirlwind of spinning air spiralling round at speeds of up to 450 km/h (280 mph). It forms during a storm and can leave a trail of incredible damage in its path.

The spiralling winds at the centre of a thundercloud rotate faster than those around the outside – in the same way that ice skaters spin faster when they pull in their arms. This central spinning column of air works its way to the ground and appears as a narrow funnel cloud.

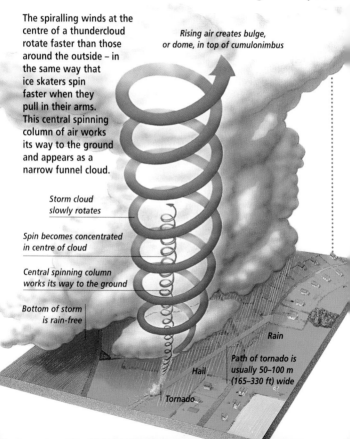

Rising air creates bulge, or dome, in top of cumulonimbus

Storm cloud slowly rotates

Spin becomes concentrated in centre of cloud

Central spinning column works its way to the ground

Bottom of storm is rain-free

Rain

Path of tornado is usually 50–100 m (165–330 ft) wide

Hail

Tornado

Most tornadoes have wind speeds of around 160 km/h (100 mph). At these speeds, nothing in the path of the tornado is safe from damage.

Twisters and dust devils

Small twisters are sometimes confused with dust devils. Dust devils are small whirlwinds that form over deserts or over bare, ploughed fields on hot sunny days. Dust devils are not attached to storm clouds like tornadoes and do not usually cause much damage.

Waterspouts

A waterspout is a tornado that occurs over the sea. Waterspouts are usually much weaker than tornadoes but they can suck up objects from the sea or beach and carry them long distances inland.

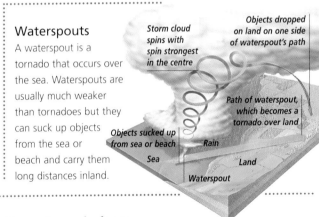

Storm cloud spins with spin strongest in the centre

Objects dropped on land on one side of waterspout's path

Path of waterspout, which becomes a tornado over land

Objects sucked up from sea or beach

Rain

Sea

Land

Waterspout

How a tornado forms

Tornadoes start when an upcurrent of air in a thundercloud is spun around by winds in the upper part of the cloud. Air is sucked into the spinning spiral at the bottom of the column and spins faster towards the centre of the column. This makes the upcurrent stronger and the column grows, reaching down from the cloud to the ground.

Tornado damage

Just one in a thousand thunderstorms produces a tornado and few tornadoes last for more than 15 minutes. Severe tornado damage is usually caused when several tornadoes occurr one after the other.

In a tornado's path

A tornado's path is usually quite narrow – sometimes as little as 50 m (165 ft) wide. Damage occurs only in this narrow strip where the tornado touches the ground. Buildings and vehicles outside the path of the tornado may be left untouched or damaged only slightly by falling debris, but buildings in the tornado's path may be completely destroyed. As it whirls over the ground, the spinning air funnel acts a bit like a vacuum cleaner, sucking up everything in its path. Lighter objects and debris may be carried up into the funnel and dropped some distance away. Heavier objects may be seriously damaged.

Some tornadoes are so powerful they can tear the roofs off buildings, smash sheds and mobile homes, and topple trucks and cars. Buildings directly in the path of a severe tornado may be completely flattened.

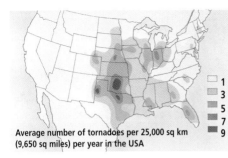

Average number of tornadoes per 25,000 sq km
(9,650 sq miles) per year in the USA

1
3
5
7
9

The United States has around 1,000 tornadoes a year. Most occur in the Great Plains, in the Midwest.

Tornado Alley

Tornadoes occur all over the world but they are most frequent in the Midwest of the United States. Part of this region has so many tornadoes it is known as Tornado Alley. Tornadoes there kill, on average, around 200 people every year.

Tornado tales

A tornado's power can produce some strange effects. Feathers have been plucked from chickens, bark from trees, and frogs and fish have been sucked up from ponds and carried several kilometres (miles). In 1981 in Italy, it was reported that a baby was lifted from its pram, carried 15 m (50 ft) into the air, then set down safely 90 m (300 ft) away – without waking up!

Tornado alert

In the United States, a tornado watch is started for areas where tornadoes are likely to occur over the next few hours. If a tornado is spotted, a tornado warning is sent out and a siren may be sounded to warn people to take shelter.

TOTO (the Totable Tornado Observatory) was built to collect information inside tornadoes.

Hurricanes

Hurricanes are the most severe and powerful storms of all. These storms are called hurricanes if they form in the Atlantic Ocean, tropical cyclones if they form around India and Australia, and typhoons if they form in the western Pacific.

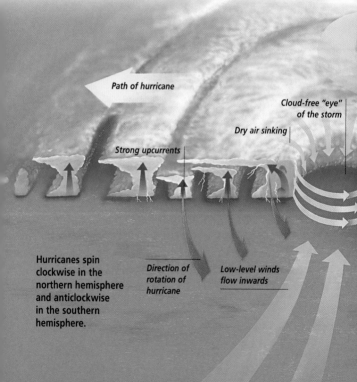

Path of hurricane

Cloud-free "eye" of the storm

Dry air sinking

Strong upcurrents

Hurricanes spin clockwise in the northern hemisphere and anticlockwise in the southern hemisphere.

Direction of rotation of hurricane

Low-level winds flow inwards

Storm surges

Fast-blowing hurricane-force winds can raise the sea level by about 1 m (3 ft) beneath the "eye", creating a huge mound of water. As a hurricane moves to the coast, the mound of water piles up against the land, and a destructive surge of water can rip boats from moorings and batter buildings.

Storm surge

Rotation of hurricane

Low pressure in "eye"

Raised dome of water beneath "eye"

If they happen at high tide, storm surges can be 3–6 m (10–20 ft) high and can cause immense damage to buildings on the coast.

How a hurricane forms

Hurricanes form over warm tropical seas when winds from opposite directions meet and begin to spiral upwards over an area of low pressure. Water vapour, carried from the sea below, rises, becomes warm and forms clouds. As the air becomes warmer, it rises more quickly. This updraft of air starts to suck in more air at the bottom and begins to spiral faster and faster. Wind speeds in severe storms can reach up to 320 km/h (200 mph), yet in the centre of the storm (called the "eye"), there is a quiet, still area, with only light winds. Hurricanes only die out over land (where there is no water vapour to fuel the storm), but it is over land that they do most damage.

Upper level winds flow outwards

Spiral of thunderstorms

Trade winds are drawn into storm

Spiral bands of rain

Hurricane watch

Because they can be so dangerous, every hurricane is tracked by satellite and from the ground to find out whether it is becoming stronger or weaker and to work out which way it is moving.

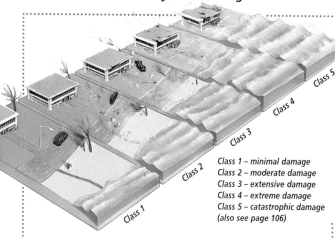

Class 5

Class 4

Class 3

Class 2

Class 1

Class 1 – minimal damage
Class 2 – moderate damage
Class 3 – extensive damage
Class 4 – extreme damage
Class 5 – catastrophic damage
(also see page 106)

Hurricane numbers

Each hurricane is given a number according to how damaging it may be. This helps people living in a danger area to plan whether to simply board up their homes or whether to leave until the danger has passed. Class 4 and 5 hurricanes are the most powerful and the ones that people fear the most. Hurricane Andrew, which hit Florida and Louisiana in the United States in August 1992, was a class 4 hurricane. High winds damaged over 125,000 homes and 61 people died.

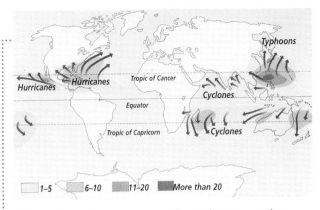

1-5   6-10   11-20   More than 20

This map shows the average number of tropical storms occurring over a 20-year period. Typical storm paths are in red.

Hurricane names

Hurricanes are given names so that everyone knows which storm is being talked about on the news or in hurricane watches. The first hurricane of the year is given a name starting with A, the next B, and so on. Most names are reused every 6 years but if a hurricane is very severe its name is "retired" and not reused for at least 10 years. An example is Hugo, which hit Puerto Rico in the Caribbean then Carolina in the United States in 1989, killing 82 people.

Watches and warning

In the United States, a hurricane watch is issued for a 480-km (300-mile) stretch of coastline when a hurricane is 36 hours away from land. Everyone there then listens for a hurricane warning, which may tell them to leave the area. Warnings need to be given a day in advance to give people time to prepare.

Damage caused by Hurricane Mitch, which hit Honduras in 1998.

Monsoons

Monsoon is the name given to the yearly winds that bring torrential rain and flooding to the tropics – especially in India (see graph on page 33) and Southeast Asia – during the summer.

Monsoon season

The word "monsoon" comes from the Arabic *mausim*, meaning season, and was first used by Arab sailors to describe the seasonal winds that blow across the Arabian Sea. The monsoon occurs in parts of Asia, Australia and Africa. As Asia is so big, its monsoon is the strongest and affects the most people.

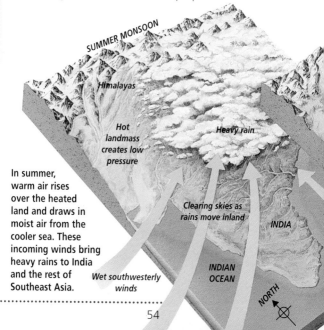

SUMMER MONSOON

Himalayas

Hot landmass creates low pressure

Heavy rain

Clearing skies as rains move inland

INDIA

INDIAN OCEAN

Wet southwesterly winds

NORTH

In summer, warm air rises over the heated land and draws in moist air from the cooler sea. These incoming winds bring heavy rains to India and the rest of Southeast Asia.

Life-giving rain

The yearly monsoon brings rain to areas that have been so hot and dry the soil bakes and the wells run dry. People greet the life-giving monsoon rains with joy, but sometimes the rains are too heavy. Floods can wash away crops and homes, and overcrowding in the region makes the damage worse.

Monsoon rains in Nepal

In winter, India and the rest of Southeast Asia become cooler. Dry chilly winds blow outwards from Asia. These winds gather warmth and moisture from the sea (which is now warmer than the land) and carry rains to the northern parts of Australia.

Himalayas

Cold landmass creates high pressure

No rain

INDIAN OCEAN

Dry northeasterly winds

INDIA

INDIAN OCEAN

WINTER MONSOON

Wet southwesterly winds

El Niño

El Niño is the name given to the dramatic changes in weather that occur every few years when warm water and a wet climate shift from the western to the eastern Pacific Ocean, and the seasonal trade winds are reversed.

Drought and flooding

El Niño (meaning "boy" in Spanish) affects rainfall, temperature and the path of tropical storms all around the world. During El Niño, Australia, Borneo and Indonesia on the western side of the Pacific suffer drought, and India and China receive less monsoon rain. Meanwhile, torrential rains hit Peru and Ecuador in South America and California in the United States.

Heavy rains brought by El Niño in January 1998 caused severe flooding in Peru.

Weather upheaval

When the eastern Pacific area has cold seas and a dry climate, it is known as La Niña (meaning "girl" in Spanish). During La Niña, cold water rising from deep ocean currents chills the air above it and brings drought. Meanwhile, in the western Pacific, the waters are warm and the climate is wet. During El Niño, the warm waters bring a wet climate to the eastern Pacific, heavy rains to the western Pacific, and severe drought in Australia.

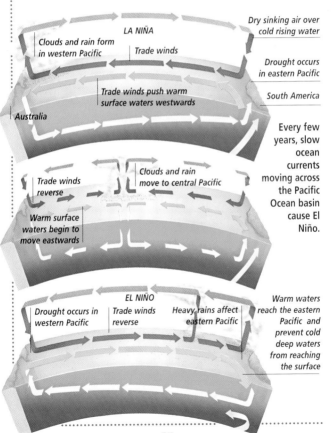

LA NIÑA

Clouds and rain form in western Pacific

Trade winds

Dry sinking air over cold rising water

Drought occurs in eastern Pacific

Trade winds push warm surface waters westwards

South America

Australia

Trade winds reverse

Clouds and rain move to central Pacific

Warm surface waters begin to move eastwards

Every few years, slow ocean currents moving across the Pacific Ocean basin cause El Niño.

EL NIÑO

Drought occurs in western Pacific

Trade winds reverse

Heavy rains affect eastern Pacific

Warm waters reach the eastern Pacific and prevent cold deep waters from reaching the surface

Flash floods

Flash floods occur when severe rain from a thunderstorm falls over mountains in a short space of time, resulting in a wall of water rushing down the mountain slopes into the valley bottom.

During a severe downburst, little rain has time to soak into the ground. Stream levels rise until a raging torrent of water rushes down the mountain slopes, carrying stones and boulders and uprooting trees.

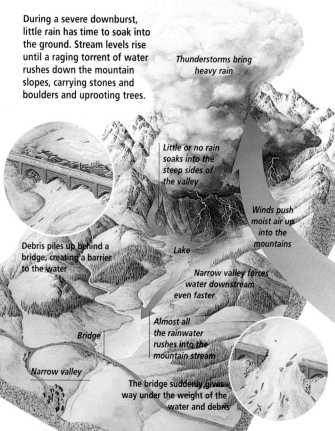

Thunderstorms bring heavy rain

Little or no rain soaks into the steep sides of the valley

Winds push moist air up into the mountains

Debris piles up behind a bridge, creating a barrier to the water

Lake

Narrow valley forces water downstream even faster

Bridge

Almost all the rainwater rushes into the mountain stream

Narrow valley

The bridge suddenly gives way under the weight of the water and debris

Protection against river flooding

River floods are slower to develop than flash floods. They are often seasonal and are caused by long periods of heavy rainfall or by the melting of deep snow over large river basins. Warnings can usually be given several hours or even days before a river is likely to burst its banks and cause damage. In areas where river flooding is a problem, different methods are tried to help to reduce the dangers and damage. Dams are sometimes built to hold back flood waters and release them more slowly. Trees planted on slopes can also slow water running downhill and give it time to seep into the earth.

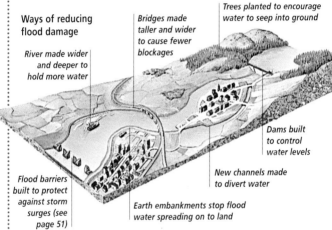

Ways of reducing flood damage

Trees planted to encourage water to seep into ground

Bridges made taller and wider to cause fewer blockages

River made wider and deeper to hold more water

Dams built to control water levels

New channels made to divert water

Flood barriers built to protect against storm surges (see page 51)

Earth embankments stop flood water spreading on to land

Wall of water

Flash floods happen so quickly that seconds count. Meteorologists attempt to give warnings by measuring the amount of rainfall in severe thunderstorms by radar. If a flash flood is likely to develop, people in the danger zone can be warned by radio, TV broadcasts, sirens or even police megaphones. Just 15 to 20 minutes' warning may be enough for people to escape to higher ground out of the path of the rushing water. Even though flash floods only affect a small area, they can be devastating and cause many deaths.

Deep freezes

Snow can make the countryside look very beautiful and can be fun for all kinds of winter sports, from sledging and skiing to building a snowman, but cold spells can also cause damage and disruption.

Blizzards

A blizzard is the name given to a combination of heavy snow, strong winds and freezing temperatures. During a blizzard, visibility is extremely poor, making it difficult and dangerous to drive. Planes may be grounded, traffic may come to a halt and power lines may collapse, leaving people without heating and light. Sometimes, people die from the cold or from traffic accidents caused by the bad weather.

In January 1998, severe ice storms in Quebec, Canada, damaged power lines and cut off heating supplies to thousands of homes.

Avalanche

An avalanche can be started by a heavy fall of snow, a slight thaw in the snow, a gust of wind, or even by the noise or movement of someone skiing in the mountains. In loose snow avalanches, the snow sweeps downhill in a rush, rather like sand being poured out of a bucket. In a slab avalanche, the snow falls in a great slab or mass. This happens when the grains of snow are tightly compacted, or squashed, together.

An avalanche may reach speeds of up to 320 km/h (200 mph).

Avalanche protection

In mountainous areas where avalanches are a threat, people build fences and walls, mound up earth or plant trees to try to hold back or slow down the snow. Fences may be positioned in a triangle to try to divert snow around a building. Some buildings are even designed in the shape of the bow of a ship so the snow sweeps past.

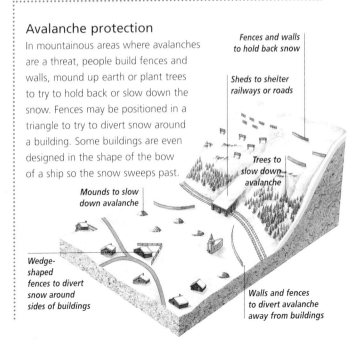

Fences and walls to hold back snow

Sheds to shelter railways or roads

Trees to slow down avalanche

Mounds to slow down avalanche

Wedge-shaped fences to divert snow around sides of buildings

Walls and fences to divert avalanche away from buildings

Drought

A drought is a period of unusual dryness when the rains fail. Drought can happen in areas that normally receive a lot of rainfall, not just in regions that expect a yearly dry season.

A blocking high (see below right) can divert storms that normally bring rain, causing water supplies to run low and crops to fail.

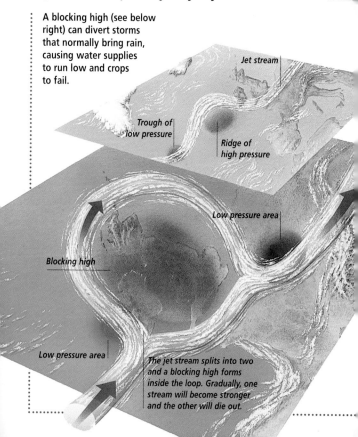

Jet stream

Trough of low pressure

Ridge of high pressure

Low pressure area

Blocking high

Low pressure area

The jet stream splits into two and a blocking high forms inside the loop. Gradually, one stream will become stronger and the other will die out.

Wildfires

Forest fires may be sparked during long periods of drought when trees and other plants are dry and burn easily. Sometimes pieces of burning bark may be carried on dry winds, sparking a new wildfire elsewhere.

Australia often has severe wildfires because the oils found in the local eucalyptus trees help to fuel the flames.

Long-term drought

Some of the world's deserts have not seen rain for many years, but this is normal. In other places, such as the Sahel region along the southern edge of the Sahara Desert in Africa, there have been long, abnormal periods of drought for around 40 years. Crops wither and famine has caused hunger and misery for millions of people.

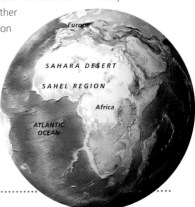

Europe

SAHARA DESERT

SAHEL REGION

Africa

ATLANTIC OCEAN

When the rains fail

The frontal depressions, or lows, that form in the tropics are steered by a jet stream (see pages 28–29). If the jet stream curves around in a loop, the lows loop too. A large anticyclone, called a blocking high, forms inside the loop. The blocking high brings clear skies and hot dry weather in summer, but if it lasts for many weeks it can cause drought.

Weather forecasting

Satellite tracking of Hurricane Mitch, October 1998 – accurately predicting the weather is a constant challenge to meteorologists.

Why make forecasts?

Knowing what the weather will be like helps us all to plan. This is particularly important for people whose work and livelihoods are greatly affected by the weather, such as farmers and fishermen.

Weather planning

Providing they are accurate, weather forecasts can help to make our lives safer and more comfortable. Most people listen to general weather forecasts on radio and television or read weather reports in newspapers and magazines. People whose work is greatly affected by the weather may pay weather agencies to supply detailed up-to-date weather reports so that they can plan.

Local authorities can salt and grit roads if they know that severe ice and snow are expected

Fishing boats and cargo ships can change route or seek shelter to avoid strong winds and storms

Supermarkets and other shops can adjust their stocks of food or clothing and rearrange displays according to weather forecasts

Weather warnings

Severe weather, such as dense fog, heavy snow or rain, ice and strong winds, can make roads dangerous and cause accidents. Local authorities need accurate forecasts so they know when to grit or even close roads.

Grit helps tyres to grip and salt can stop ice forming or make it melt.

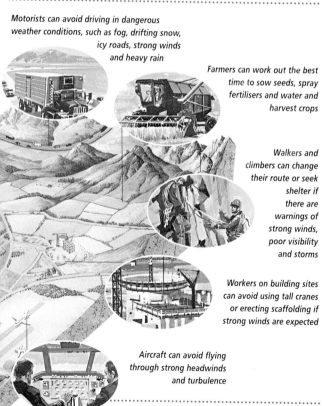

Motorists can avoid driving in dangerous weather conditions, such as fog, drifting snow, icy roads, strong winds and heavy rain

Farmers can work out the best time to sow seeds, spray fertilisers and water and harvest crops

Walkers and climbers can change their route or seek shelter if there are warnings of strong winds, poor visibility and storms

Workers on building sites can avoid using tall cranes or erecting scaffolding if strong winds are expected

Aircraft can avoid flying through strong headwinds and turbulence

Weather stations

Every three hours, millions of weather observations are sent to international weather centres to make forecasts and maps.

Collecting information

Meteorologists all over the world use standard instruments to record weather conditions so that the information can be compared. A white wooden shelter, called a Stevenson screen, protects the instruments from direct sunlight and allows air to circulate freely inside.

Rain gauge measures precipitation

Dry-bulb thermometer measures air temperature

Simple wet-bulb thermometer measures humidity

Simple barometer measures air pressure

Thermograph records temperature changes on a paper chart

Minimum thermometer records how low the temperature falls

Maximum thermometer records how high the temperature rises

Shelter holds instruments 1.2 m (4 ft) above the ground

Radiosonde balloons are sent up into the atmosphere from around 700 weather stations worldwide each day.

Atmospheric conditions

Weather conditions in the upper atmosphere are measured by weather planes and by radiosonde balloons. Each balloon is tracked to measure wind speed and direction. As they rise, the balloons send back information by radio.

Making observations

Meteorologists record information about each element of the weather – cloud cover and type of cloud, temperature, hours of sunshine, humidity, wind strength and direction, air pressure, visibility and precipitation. Precipitation is always recorded as the depth of water collected in a rain gauge, even if the water is melted snow, sleet or hail. A snow depth of about 120 mm (5 in) melts to around 10 mm (⅜ in) of water.

Clouds

Temperature

Sunshine

Humidity

Wind strength and direction

Air pressure

Visibility

Precipitation (rain or snow)

Eyes on
the world

High above the Earth's surface, remote-sensing equipment on board weather satellites provides invaluable information on global weather systems, such as cloud formations and hurricanes.

Weather satellites

There are two types of weather satellites. Geostationary satellites remain in the same spot above the Earth's surface and send back images that can scan nearly half the planet every 30 minutes. Polar orbiting satellites travel from pole to pole. They scan a different area of the Earth every two hours or so, passing over the same places on Earth twice a day.

Information gathered by satellites has made weather forecasting more accurate. Storms can be photographed and measurements taken.

On-screen monitoring

Readings from instruments on board satellites are monitored at weather stations, where information is often displayed on computer screens.

Meteorologists have so much weather data to analyse that they need powerful supercomputers to condense the data so that it can be read and managed more easily.

A meteorologist monitors data from satellites at the Meteorological Office in Bracknell, United Kingdom.

A satellite image shows a storm over the Bering Sea, coloured by a computer to pick out the clouds.

Satellite images

Satellites carry two types of sensors. One is an imager, or visible light sensor, which works like a camera. It can only be used during the day because it works by using reflected light. The other is a sounder, or infrared sensor. This reads the temperature of the clouds or air. Infrared sensors can be used at night as well as during the day.

In this satellite image of Hurricane Gilbert, warm land shows up black or dark grey and cooler cloud tops as white or light grey.

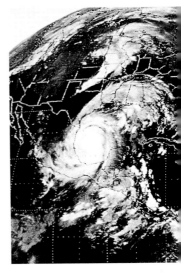

Forecasting the weather

Modern weather forecasting involves using a combination of data from observations, balloons and satellites together with computer models and a knowledge of weather trends and patterns.

⟍⟍ *Nimbostratus*

● *Full cloud cover*

∴ *Continuous rain*

◣ *Wind speed 60 knots (111 km/h or 70 mph); temperature 14°C (57°F)*

◸ *Cumulonimbus*

● *Full cloud cover*

⋮ *Heavy intermittent rain*

◟⟍ *Wind speed 30 knots (56 km/h or 35 mph); temperature 11°C (51°F)*

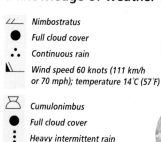

Making weather forecasts

The next day's weather forecast is made up from information fed into a supercomputer which works out how air pressure, winds, temperature and moisture are likely to change over the next

⟜○⟝ *Stratocumulus*

◐ *Half cloud cover*

⟍ *Wind speed 15 knots (28 km/h or 17 mph); temperature 18°C (64°F)*

10 minutes. Weather predictions based on this short forecast are fed into another computer which works out a further forecast, and so on, up to 24 hours. Although it is possible to make accurate five-day forecasts, long-range forecasts are almost impossible because of the complexity of Earth's weather systems.

Television weather forecasts (here, from Britain's BBC) often use their own easily understood weather symbols.

⌒ Hook-shaped cirrus

◑ Half cloud cover

⟍ Wind speed 15 knots
(28 km/h or 17 mph);
temperature 15°C (59°F)

Weather symbols

Forecasters use standard weather symbols so that they can exchange information easily. Turn to pages 110–111 for the meanings of some international weather symbols.

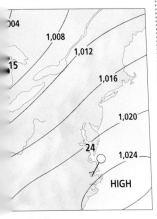

○ No cloud

⟍ Light winds
5 knots (9 km/h or 5 mph);
temperature 24°C (75°F)

Reading weather maps

The lines shown on a weather map are called isobars. They are used to join up areas with the same air pressure. Generally, the closer together the isobars, the stronger the winds. Air pressure along each isobar is given in millibars (average air pressure on the Earth's surface is 1,013 millibars).

Areas enclosed by isobars are areas of high or low pressure. The weather fronts at a low (shown by thick curved lines) produce particular weather conditions. Wind speed is measured in knots. The wind symbol is drawn pointing towards the cloud cover symbol in the direction in which the wind is blowing.

73

Skywatching

You don't need your own weather station to forecast the weather. Just watching the sky can give clues about what is happening in the atmosphere and how the weather may change.

Blues skies

White light from the Sun is made up of the colours of the rainbow. As sunlight travels through the atmosphere, it strikes water droplets, ice crystals or particles of dust and pollution. These scatter the light and make it (and the colours it contains) behave in particular ways. Blue in sunlight is scattered the most, creating a brilliant blue sky on warm sunny days.

The sky is deep blue when the air is cold, dry and clean with no pollutants present in the atmosphere.

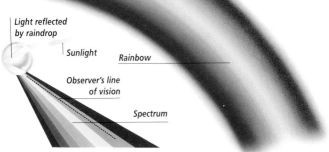

Light reflected by raindrop

Sunlight

Rainbow

Observer's line of vision

Spectrum

Rainbow lights

Rainbows form when sunlight from behind you is split into the colours of the spectrum as it passes through raindrops. Because weather usually moves from west to east, a rainbow seen to the east in the afternoon or evening may indicate that good weather is on its way. A morning rainbow in the west may indicate coming rain.

Red skies

The sky at sunset and sunrise oftens turns a brilliant red. This happens because the Sun is low in the sky and sunlight has to travel a longer distance through the atmosphere. This splits and scatters the light. Blue light is scattered most, so only red, orange and yellow are left by the time the light reaches the ground and we see an orangey-red sky.

In Britain, a red sky in the evening is thought to be a sign that good weather is coming. This is because most weather blows in from the west and a red sunset indicates the western sky is clear.

Sun

At midday, light travels through less atmosphere

Atmosphere

At sunrise and sunset, light travels farther through atmosphere

Sun

75

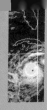

Cloudwatching

Clouds can also give us clues about the weather. Simply knowing that clouds are blown by winds tells us from which direction weather is coming.

Fair-weather cumulus

Deep rain-bearing cumulus

Cumulonimbus, or storm clouds

Will it rain?

Whether or not it will rain can often be seen from the sky and the clouds. A few hours before rain arrives on a warm front, distant objects stand out and look brightly coloured. This is because dry polar air often moves ahead of a warm front. The polar air is unusually clear and cold and gives good visibility. Elongated cumulus, called fair-weather cumulus, usually indicate that finer weather is on the way, but if cauliflower-shaped bulges start growing from the cloud-tops, showers may develop in the afternoon. Deep cumulus are more likely to produce rain than shallow clouds because they contain more water. Deeper clouds usually have grey bases because sunlight cannot pass through the water they contain. Deep, dark cumulonimbus mean plenty of rain and possibly storms.

Contrails

The streaky white cirrus clouds trailing behind aircraft are called condensation trails, or contrails. They are formed when water vapour from an aircraft's jet exhausts forms ice crystals in the high-altitude freezing air.

Short contrails indicate dry weather as they are evaporating quickly. Long contrails occur in moist air and may indicate changeable weather.

Clouds shapes sometimes show movement in the atmosphere.

Making waves

Sometimes clouds make fantastic shapes in the sky. Occasionally, you may see cloud waves, which are formed when the wind is travelling at different speeds in adjacent layers of the atmosphere.

Lenticular clouds

Sometimes waves develop in winds as they blow over a mountain range. Smooth lens-shaped clouds, called lenticular clouds, form at the tops of the waves where the air rises, cools and condenses into water droplets. Lenticular clouds often hang in the same spot for a long time because they are "fixed" to the waves.

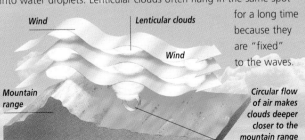

Wind | *Lenticular clouds*

Wind

Mountain range

Circular flow of air makes clouds deeper closer to the mountain range

Weather lore

Over the centuries, people have passed down a store of weather knowledge, often in the form of short rhymes or sayings. Most of these scraps of weather lore cannot be used for accurate predictions, but some are generally reliable.

Traditional rhymes and sayings

In the middle latitudes, where weather fronts bring bands of rain, people may say "Rain before seven, fine before eleven". This rhyme is generally true because most rain bands are 260–320 km (160–200 miles) wide and move at about 65 km/h (40 mph) so they last for four or five hours. Sayings about the wind such as "The north wind doth blow, and we shall have snow" are less reliable and may only be true for particular areas or places.

A deep red evening sky with dark clouds may indicate rain in the morning – the opposite of the familiar weather rhyme, "Red sky at night, shepherds' delight; Red sky at morning, shepherds' warning."

Weather wisdom

People look at signs in nature for clues about the weather. Some plants, such as morning glory, close their flowers when the air becomes damp, indicating coming rain. Seaweed is often a good indicator of the weather, too. Many types of seaweed become damp and slimy when the air is humid, suggesting that rain may follow. Larch pine cones also open or close according to changes in humidity. Other local lore, such as the saying that sheep and cows lie down when rain is coming, has less basis in scientific fact – perhaps the animals simply want a dry place to rest.

Seaweed becomes dry in dry air.

Cones close in wet weather.

Cones open in dry weather.

Weather houses

In some parts of Europe, small weather houses were made to forecast whether it would rain. Inside the house, two figures were fixed to a wooden platform which, in turn, was attached to a hair. As hair expands in damp weather and contracts in dry weather, changes in the hair moved the platform and the figures attached to it.

A tiny figure of a man or woman comes out of one of the doors of the weather house depending on whether the air is humid or dry.

A changing climate

Burning fuel to produce electricity results in large quantities of carbon dioxide – the main greenhouse gas – polluting the atmosphere.

Clues to the past

The Earth's climate changes slowly over the centuries. Studying its past climate may help us understand how the climate may change in the future.

Ammonite fossil

How we can tell

The scientific study of weather and climate only began around 300 years ago. To learn about climate thousands or even millions of years ago, scientists must look for clues. Some climate clues are found in the fossilised remains of plants and animals, because living organisms adapt to the climate in which they live.

A fish dies and decays on the seabed, leaving hard bones and teeth.

Over millions of years, the bones and teeth become fossilised.

The fossil is slowly exposed by erosion and land movement.

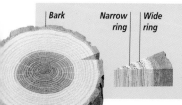

Bark	Narrow ring	Wide ring

A tree adds a new ring of wood to its trunk every year – a narrow ring in dry years and a thick ring in wet years. By studying tree rings, scientists have built up a record of climate change over 8,000 years.

Historical evidence

Clues about changes in climate also come from ships' logs, weather diaries or records of wine harvests. Paintings give us pictures of weather conditions, too. Many paintings show that deep winter snows were common in northern Europe during the 16th century.

Winter Scene painted by Pieter Brueghel (around 1515–69).

Dramatic climate change

Some climate changes are slight, for example with dry summers or mild winters becoming a little more frequent. Other changes are dramatic. Many scientists believe that around 65 million years ago, an asteroid struck the Earth, causing a massive change in climate and killing off three-quarters of all forms of life, including the dinosaurs.

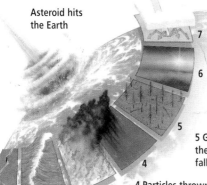

Asteroid hits the Earth

7 A "greenhouse" warming of the Earth's climate might have followed.

6 Dust would have blocked out the Sun's heat and light.

5 Gases produced in the impact would have fallen as acid rain.

4 Particles thrown into the atmosphere would have fallen over a huge area.

1 Stress on the Earth's crust would have triggered earthquakes.

2 Tsunamis (tidal waves) would have been caused by underwater earthquakes.

3 Energy released by the impact would have resulted in huge forest fires.

The ice ages

At several periods during the past 2 million years, ice has covered large areas of the Earth's land. We call these periods ice ages, or glacials. The last ice age ended around 10,000 years ago.

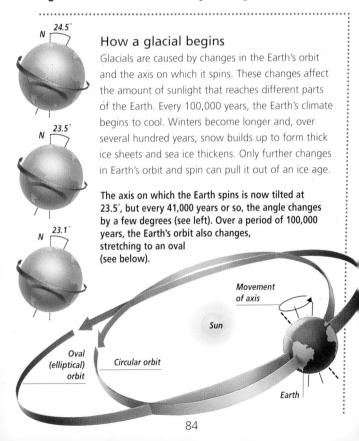

How a glacial begins

Glacials are caused by changes in the Earth's orbit and the axis on which it spins. These changes affect the amount of sunlight that reaches different parts of the Earth. Every 100,000 years, the Earth's climate begins to cool. Winters become longer and, over several hundred years, snow builds up to form thick ice sheets and sea ice thickens. Only further changes in Earth's orbit and spin can pull it out of an ice age.

The axis on which the Earth spins is now tilted at 23.5°, but every 41,000 years or so, the angle changes by a few degrees (see left). Over a period of 100,000 years, the Earth's orbit also changes, stretching to an oval (see below).

N 24.5°

N 23.5°

N 23.1°

Movement of axis

Sun

Oval (elliptical) orbit

Circular orbit

Earth

Interglacials

Interglacial is the name given to the warmer climate conditions between glacials – such as the climate we enjoy today. At present, large ice sheets are found only in Greenland and Antarctica. However, the last glacial has left its mark on the land, with the weight of slowly advancing ice carving out new valleys and lakes in the Earth's surface.

An icebreaker carves a path through Antarctic sea ice.

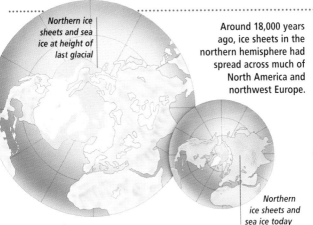

Northern ice sheets and sea ice at height of last glacial

Around 18,000 years ago, ice sheets in the northern hemisphere had spread across much of North America and northwest Europe.

Northern ice sheets and sea ice today

Ice age climate

At the height of the last glacial, around 18,000 years ago, northern Europe, parts of Siberia, Canada, northern parts of the United States, New Zealand, Tasmania and the tip of South America were covered by thick ice sheets, some up to 1,000 m (3,300 ft) deep. Seawater froze, making the sea level fall by 100 m (330 ft), and coastlines extended into the sea so that islands like Britain were linked to Europe by land.

Darkness and light

When a volcano erupts, it throws huge amounts of debris, such as dust, ash, smoke and gases, into the atmosphere. Sometimes, this debris can block out the Sun's light, cooling the Earth's climate.

Cooling the climate

Heavy ash thrown into the troposphere (the layer of atmosphere nearest Earth's surface) by a major eruption is usually washed back to Earth by precipitation within a few weeks. However, fine dust and gases may reach the stratosphere and be spread around the Earth by high-level winds. This material acts like a sunscreen, blocking out some of the Sun's light, and may cool the climate for up to three years, bringing chilly winters and cool summers.

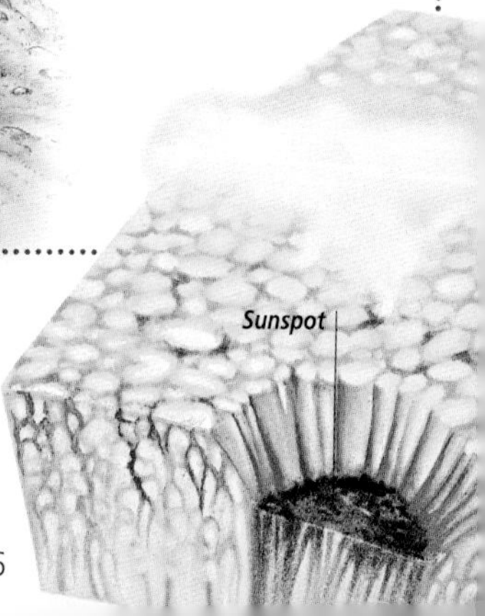

Sunspots on the Sun's surface (shown here close-up) follow a cycle from many to few every 11 years. Some scientists believe this cycle affects the pattern of drought, rainfall and cool winters in different parts of the Earth.

Sunspot

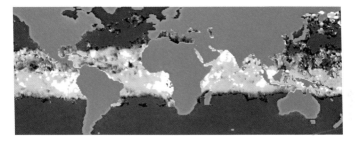

Satellite images taken immediately after the eruption of Mount Pinatubo (top) and two months later (bottom) show how winds have spread dust and gas (shown in yellow and white) around the equator.

Cool and cold

When Mount Pinatubo erupted in the Philippines in June 1991, it blasted 15 million tonnes (tons) of dust and gas high into the stratosphere. This blocked out some of the Sun's light and, within a year, the average global temperature dropped by 5°C (9°F). Some regions cooled more than others, affecting world winds and storm tracks.

Sunspot

Sunspots

Dark patches observed on the surface of the Sun are called sunspots. Many sunspots indicate that the Sun is hotter and more active than usual. Fewer sunspots indicate a weaker, cooler Sun. When the Sun's light is strong the Earth may become warmer; when it is weak the Earth may cool.

Pollution

Every day, exhaust fumes from millions of vehicles and smoke and acid gases from factory chimneys are being pumped into the air. These pollutants change the atmosphere and our climate.

City smog

Pollutants released from cars and factory chimneys in cities can create a thick brownish smog. Smog often forms on calm days in an area of high pressure, when sinking air stops pollutants escaping into the atmosphere. Sometimes smog warnings are given out. These are particularly vital to people with breathing difficulties, such as asthma, which can be made worse by choking smog.

A thick smog obscures the mountains behind Mexico City (above), the world's most polluted city.

A child with asthma (right) uses a respirator to help him breathe more easily.

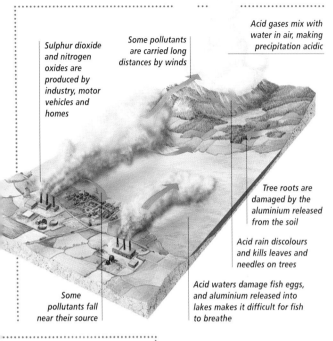

Sulphur dioxide and nitrogen oxides are produced by industry, motor vehicles and homes

Some pollutants are carried long distances by winds

Acid gases mix with water in air, making precipitation acidic

Tree roots are damaged by the aluminium released from the soil

Acid rain discolours and kills leaves and needles on trees

Acid waters damage fish eggs, and aluminium released into lakes makes it difficult for fish to breathe

Some pollutants fall near their source

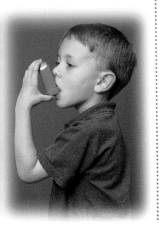

Acid rain

When oil and coal are burned, they release gases. Some of these gases, such as sulphur dioxide and nitrogen oxides, mix with the moisture in the air and make it acidic. Acid rain is harmful to animals and plants. It washes nutrients from the soil and from leaves and needles. It also releases aluminium, which is usually locked up in the soil. This aluminium washes into lakes and rivers, eventually killing fish.

89

The ozone hole

Human activities are severely damaging the ozone layer, part of the shield of gases in the atmosphere that protects the Earth from the Sun's harmful rays.

The ozone balance

Ozone, a bluish gas, is a form of oxygen. The amount of ozone in the atmosphere remained more or less the same for millions of years until the 1960s, when huge quantities of CFCs, or chlorofluorocarbons, were released into the atmosphere, attacking and breaking down the ozone layer. CFCs remain in the atmosphere for up to 140 years so their effect on the ozone layer continues. Large "holes" in the ozone layer have been found above the Arctic, Australia and New Zealand, with the most dramatic over Antarctica.

Ultraviolet rays from the Sun pass through "holes" in the ozone layer, where the ozone gases are thinner. Thinning of the ozone layer is mainly caused by CFCs used in refrigerator cooling systems, air conditioning units, some spray cans and some types of packaging.

Sun

Ozone layer stops most ultraviolet rays from the Sun

Thinning of ozone layer

Antarctic ozone hole

Scientists began measuring the amount of ozone in the ozone layer in the 1960s. During the early 1980s, they discovered that it thins dramatically above the Antarctic every year from September to October, forming a "hole" around 1.5 times the size of the United States.

The ozone hole (shown in pale blue) over Antarctica (darker blue) at its 1999 maximum of 25 million sq km (9.8 million sq miles).

Ultraviolet rays

Ozone filters out most of the harmful ultraviolet rays from the Sun. Ultraviolet rays can damage eyes, cause sunburn and lead to skin cancers. If the ozone layer is thinned further, these health hazards may become much worse. Some scientists also believe that infectious diseases may be spread more quickly.

Wearing hats and sunscreen lotion can help to protect against sunburn caused by the Sun's ultraviolet rays.

A buildup of some gases in the atmosphere stops heat escaping from the Earth and may be the cause of global warming *(see pages 92–93)*

Greenhouse effect

The Earth's climate is slowly getting warmer. Many scientists believe that increased global temperatures are due to the greenhouse effect.

Sunlight reflected off clouds

What is the greenhouse effect?

Greenhouse gases act in the same way as the panes of glass in a greenhouse – they let sunlight and heat in but stop heat getting out. If we didn't have greenhouse gases, the Earth's average temperature would be a cold −17°C (0°F) instead of 15°C (59°F), so they are important for our survival. What concerns scientists, however, is the increasing amount of greenhouse gases that will be produced in the future. Around half of the greenhouse gases that enter the Earth's atmosphere remain there. This means that the amount of greenhouse gases is increasing and the Earth's climate will continue to warm.

Methane from animals' digestion, swamps, rotting vegetation and gas pipes

CFCs from some spray cans, foam plastics and old refrigerator systems

Methane from rotting rubbish and refuse

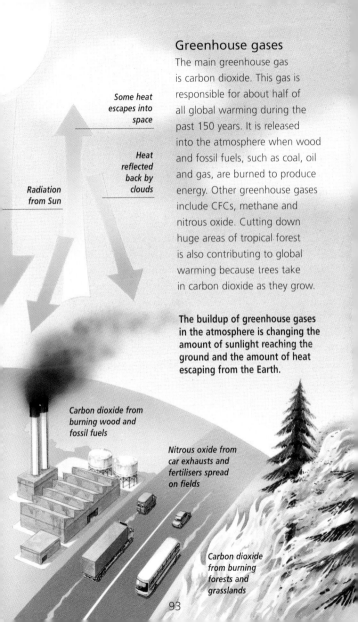

Greenhouse gases

The main greenhouse gas is carbon dioxide. This gas is responsible for about half of all global warming during the past 150 years. It is released into the atmosphere when wood and fossil fuels, such as coal, oil and gas, are burned to produce energy. Other greenhouse gases include CFCs, methane and nitrous oxide. Cutting down huge areas of tropical forest is also contributing to global warming because trees take in carbon dioxide as they grow.

The buildup of greenhouse gases in the atmosphere is changing the amount of sunlight reaching the ground and the amount of heat escaping from the Earth.

Some heat escapes into space

Heat reflected back by clouds

Radiation from Sun

Carbon dioxide from burning wood and fossil fuels

Nitrous oxide from car exhausts and fertilisers spread on fields

Carbon dioxide from burning forests and grasslands

Earth's future climate

The Earth is due for another ice age, perhaps within the next 1,000 years, yet the Earth's climate is warming because of greenhouse gases. Which trend will win?

Eco house

It is hard to predict Earth's future climate. However, it is clear that human activities need to be controlled so that we do not add to global warming. In the future, more people could live in eco-friendly houses such as the Oxford Eco House in England, which was designed to use as little energy as possible for heating, cooling, cooking and lighting.

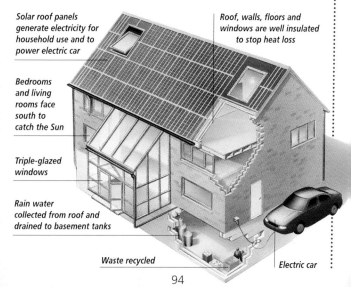

Solar roof panels generate electricity for household use and to power electric car

Roof, walls, floors and windows are well insulated to stop heat loss

Bedrooms and living rooms face south to catch the Sun

Triple-glazed windows

Rain water collected from roof and drained to basement tanks

Waste recycled

Electric car

Hotting up

Industrialised countries have agreed not to increase the amount of greenhouse gases they release into the atmosphere. However, much more drastic measures are needed to prevent further global warming. If global warming is allowed to continue, sea levels may rise between 15 and 45 cm (6 and 18 in) by 2050. Some regions will become drier; others wetter, and some plants and animals may die.

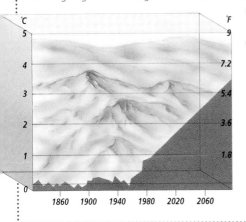

Scientists' estimates of rises in the Earth's average temperature

Renewable energy

The limited amount of fossil fuels on Earth will eventually run out. Countries need to harness renewable sources of energy, such as solar power, wave power and wind power, to replace fossil fuels and help to reduce global warming. On wind farms, wind power drives turbines to generate electrical energy. The energy produced by each turbine is proportional to the wind speed.

Experimental wind farm in Palm Springs, California, United States

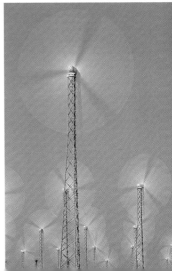

95

Fact file

· ·

· ·

Weather is happening all the time all
around the world. It is an amazing
natural phenomenon with many
extremes, from droughts to floods.

Weather records

Most weather records have remained the same for many years. A few records have been broken in the last 20 years, and some weather extremes may be broken again in the future.

TEMPERATURE AND HOURS OF SUNSHINE

Record	Temperature/Sunshine	Place	Date
Highest temperature recorded in the shade	57.8°C (136°F)	Al-Azizyah, Libya, Africa	13 September 1922
Lowest temperature	−89.2°C (−128.6°F)	Plateau Station, Antarctica	21 July 1983
Hottest place on Earth	34.4°C (93.9°F)	Dallol, Ethiopia, Africa	(Annual mean temperature)
Coldest place on Earth	−57°C (−71°F)	Antarctica	(Annual mean temperature)
Most sunshine	90% (over 4,000 hours a year)	Yuma, Arizona, USA	–
Least sunshine	Nil for 182 days	South Pole	–

The coldest place in the world is the frozen continent of Antarctica.

The hottest place in the USA, and the second-hottest place in the world, is Death Valley, California, USA.

The wettest place in the world is the Shillong Plateau area of India. Most rain falls between June and September and can reach almost 12,000 mm (472 in) a year.

RAINFALL AND HOURS OF RAIN

Record	Rainfall	Place	Date
Wettest place	11,873 mm (467 in)	Shillong Plateau, India, Asia	(Annual mean)
Driest place	0.1 mm (fraction of in)	Atacama Desert, Chile, S America	(Annual mean)
Most rainy days	Up to 350 per year	Mount Waialeale, Hawaii, USA	–
Greatest rainfall in 12 months	26,466 mm (1,042 in)	Cherrapunji, India, Asia	1 August 1860 to 31 July 1861
Highest average days of thunder	251 days per year	Tororo, Uganda, Africa	–

The driest place in the world is the Atacama Desert in Chile, South America, which has virtually no rainfall at all.

When snow falls, it can soon build up into deep snow drifts. Over a 12-month period in 1971–72, more than 30 m (100 ft) of snow fell on Mount Rainier, Washington State, USA.

SNOW AND ICE

Record	Depth/Size	Place	Date
Greatest annual snowfall	31,102 mm (1,224½ in)	Mount Rainier, Washington, USA	19 February 1971 to 18 February 1972
Heaviest hailstones	1 kg (2.2 lb)	Gopalganj, Bangladesh, Asia	14 April, 1986

NOTABLE BLIZZARDS

Date	Place	Deaths
1996	Himalayas	239
1996	Northeastern USA	100
1993	Eastern USA	200
1967	Southwestern USA	51
1958	Northeastern USA	171
1956	Western Europe	–
1947	New York City, Northeast USA	55
1940	Northeast and midwest USA	144
1888	Eastern USA	400

Millions of snowflakes fall in a single snowstorm. Every single snowflake has a different six-sided pattern.

NOTABLE FLOODS

Region	Date	Effects
Mozambique, Africa	2000	Hundreds killed
Papua New Guinea	1998	3,000 killed
Chang Jiang, China	1991	Rising river water; 1,700 killed; 2 million homeless
Bay of Bengal	1970	Storm surge, over 250,000 killed
Farahzad, Iran	1954	2,000 killed
Chang Jiang, China	1931	3,700,000 killed
Chang Jiang, China	1911	100,000 killed
Galveston, Texas, USA	1900	5,000 killed
Johnstown, Pennsylvania, USA	1889	Dam failure; 2,209 killed

In April 2000, the western Indian state of Gujarat was hit by the worst drought it had experienced in 100 years. Over 9,000 villages were seriously affected by this extreme weather.

NOTABLE DROUGHTS

Region	Date	Effects
Sahel, Sahara	1982–85, 1972–75 1940–44, 1920–14	The Sahel region has suffered from periods of devastating drought for nearly 100 years
India	1965–67	Persistent drought caused the death of around 1.5 million people
Midwestern USA	1930–37	Dry soil blown away after years of intense agriculture, creating the Dust Bowl

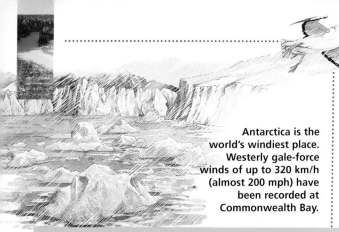

Antarctica is the world's windiest place. Westerly gale-force winds of up to 320 km/h (almost 200 mph) have been recorded at Commonwealth Bay.

WIND AND WIND SPEEDS

Record	Wind speed	Place	Date
Windiest place	322 km/h (200 mph)	Commonwealth Bay, Antarctica	(In gales)
Highest surface wind speed (high altitude)	372 km/h (231 mph)	Mt Washington, New Hampshire, USA	12 April 1934
Highest surface wind speed (low altitude)	333 km/h (207 mph)	Qaanaaq (Thule), Greenland	8 March 1972
Fastest wind speed in a tornado (measured using radar)	512 km/h (318 mph)	Oklahoma City, Oklahoma, USA	3 May 1999

AIR PRESSURE

Record	Pressure*	Place	Date
Highest barometric pressure	1,083.8 mb	Agata, Siberia, Russian Federation, Asia	31 December 1968
Lowest barometric pressure	870 mb	483 km (300 miles) west of Guam, Pacific Ocean	12 October 1979

* Earth's average air pressure is 1,013 millibars (mb)

World winds

Some names for local winds are based on the wind's direction, or whether it is cool, warm, moist or dry. Other names describe the wind's effect on the land and people.

SOME NAMES FOR LOCAL WINDS

Name	Region	Description
Blizzard	Mostly Canada and northern USA	Icy gale-force wind from the north or northwest, bringing snow
Brickfielder	Southern Australia	Hot, dry and dusty wind blowing from interior deserts; named because the wind raised dust from brick fields south of Sydney
Brisa	South America	Trade winds blowing from the northeast
Challiho	India	Strong southerly spring wind; forerunner of the monsoon
Chili	Tunisia	Hot, dry and dusty wind blowing from the deserts of North Africa
Cockeyed Bob	Northwestern Australia	Squally wind blowing mostly from December to March
Haboob	Northwest Africa	Severe summer dust storm
Mistral	Mediterranean	Cold, dry northerly wind blowing mostly in the winter and spring
Sirocco	Mediterranean	Warm spring wind blowing from the hot dry Sahara and Arabian deserts
Steppenwind	Germany	Strong cold wind blowing from the steppes region of Russia
Whirly	Antarctic	Small violent storm with whirling winds

Wind scale

In 1806, British Admiral Sir Francis Beaufort worked out this scale for estimating wind strength at sea. Effects of winds on land were added later.

BEAUFORT SCALE

No*	Name	Wind speed km/h (mph)	Effect on land
0	Calm	Under 1 (under 1)	Calm; smoke goes straight up
1	Light air	2–5 (1–3)	Smoke drifts
2	Light breeze	6–11 (4–7)	Wind felt on face, leaves rustle, ordinary weather vanes move
3	Gentle breeze	12–19 (8–12)	Leaves and small twigs in constant motion, light flag extended
4	Moderate breeze	20–28 (13–17)	Small branches move, dust and loose paper raised
5	Fresh breeze	29–38 (18–24)	Small trees sway, crested wavelets on inland waters
6	Strong breeze	39–49 (25–30)	Large branches sway, whistling heard in telegraph wires
7	Near gale	50–61 (31–38)	Whole trees sway, difficult to walk into the wind
8	Gale	62–74 (39–46)	Twigs break off trees
9	Strong gale	75–88 (47–54)	Slight damage to buildings
10	Storm	89–102 (55–63)	Trees uprooted
11	Violent storm	103–117 (64–73)	Widespread damage
12	Hurricane	Over 117 (over 73)	Buildings wrecked

* Wind speed on land is given in force numbers from 0 to 12.

Tornado scale

The Fujita–Pearson scale was developed by Dr Theodore Fujita to classify tornadoes based on wind damage.

FUJITA SCALE

No/Category	Wind speed km/h (mph)	Effect
F0	64–116 (40–72)	Chimney damage, tree branches broken
F1	117–180 (73–112)	Mobile homes pushed off their foundations or overturned
F2	181–253 (113–157)	Considerable damage; mobile homes destroyed, trees uprooted
F3	254–332 (158–206)	Roofs and walls torn down, cars thrown, trains overturned
F4	333–418 (207–260)	Well-constructed walls torn down
F5	420–512 (261–318)	Homes lifted off foundations and carried considerable distances

NOTABLE US TORNADOES

Region	Date	Deaths
Oklahoma (F5)	1999	(Low)
Southeast	1994	52
Southeast	1974	315
Midwest	1965	27
Georgia, Mississippi	1936	455
Alabama	1932	268
Midwest	1925	689

A tornado-damaged trailer park in Florida

Hurricane scale

This scale was developed by Herbert Saffir and Dr Robert Simpson in the early 1920s to measure potential hurricane damage. It is based on wind speeds and includes estimates of storm surge in each of the five catagories.

SAFFIR–SIMPSON HURRICANE DAMAGE SCALE

No/ Category	Wind speed km/h (mph)	Storm surge m (ft)	Effect on land
1 Minimal	119–153 (74–95)	1.2–1.5 (4–5)	Damage to trees and shrubs
2 Moderate	154–176 (96–110)	1.8–2.3 (6–8)	Considerable damage to trees and shrubs, some trees blown down; major damage to exposed mobile homes
3 Extensive	179–209 (111–130)	2.7–3.6 (9–12)	Large trees blown down; mobile homes destroyed; some damage to small buildings and windows, doors and roofs
4 Extreme	210–249 (131–155)	3.9–5.5 (13–18)	Trees, shrubs and signs blown down; mobile homes demolished; extensive damage to windows, doors and roofs
5 Catastrophic	Over 249 (155)	Over 5.5 (18)	All trees, shrubs and signs blown down; severe and extensive damage to buildings with some complete buildings destroyed; mobile homes demolished

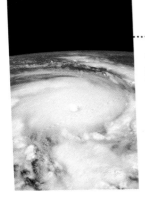

The swirling winds of Hurricane Emilia, seen from space. The "eye" in the centre of the storm provides places over which it passes a brief respite of around half an hour.

NOTABLE HURRICANES, TYPHOONS AND CYCLONES

Name/Place	Date	Deaths
Hurricane Floyd, eastern USA	1999	17
Hurricane Georges, Puerto Rico, Florida Keys, southeastern USA	1998	16
Cyclone, Andhra Pradesh, India	1996	1,000+
Hurricane Andrew, Florida, Louisiana, USA	1992	61
Cyclone, Bangladesh	1991	139,000
Hurricane Hugo, Puerto Rico, US Virgin Islands and South and North Carolina, USA	1989	86
Cyclone, Bangladesh	1970	300,000
Hurricane Flora, Caribbean	1963	6,000
Typhoon Vera, (also called the Isewan), Japan	1959	4,466
Cyclone, Bay of Bengal	1942	40,000
Typhoon, Hong Kong	1906	10,000

Effect at coast

Minor damage to piers; small craft in exposed anchorages torn from moorings

Considerable damage to piers and marinas; small craft in protected anchorages torn from moorings

Serious flooding along coast; smaller buildings near the coast destroyed

Flat land 3 m (10 ft) or less above sea level flooded inland as far as 10 km (6 miles); flooding and battering by waves and floating debris

Major damage to lower floors of all buildings less than 4.6 m (15 ft) above sea level within 457 m (1,500 ft) of the shore; massive evacuation near coast may be required

Clouds and fog

The following tables show the main types of cloud and fog. Fog is a kind of cloud with its base touching the ground.

MAIN CLOUD TYPES

Cloud layer	Description	Altitude m (ft)
Stratus	Very flat, generally uniform and grey; sun may shine through layer	Below 450 (below 1,476)
Cumulus	Fluffy cotton-wool type clouds with rounded cauliflower tops	450–2,000 (1,476–6,562)
Stratocumulus	Low-level grey or white cloud in flat layer but with rolls or rounded masses	450–2,000 (1,456–6,562)
Cumulonimbus	Towering, dense rain-bearing cumulus clouds, sometimes with anvil-shaped top	450–2,000 (1,456–6,562)
Nimbostratus*	Thick grey or dark grey layers of rain- or snow-bearing cloud	900–3,000 (2,953–9,842)
Altostratus	Mid-altitude clouds with a flat, sheetlike shape	2,000–7,000 (6,562–22,966)
Altocumulus	Mid-altitude white or grey layered clouds with rounded cumulus shapes	2,000–7,000 (6,562–22,966)
Cirrus	High-level detatched clouds made up of ice crystals; often semi-transparent	5,000–13,500 (16,404–44,291)
Cirrostratus	Whitish cirrus clouds with a smooth and flat sheetlike appearance	5,000–13,500 (16,404–44,291)
Cirrocumulus	Cirrus clouds with small cumulus shapes looking like ripples or grains	5,000–13,500 (16,404–44,291)

* Nimbostratus can extend to other levels

FOG VISIBILITY

Fog	Visibility m (ft)	Effects
Fog	below 1,000 (3,300)	Disrupts aircraft
Thick fog	50–200 (165–656)	Dangerous for road traffic
Dense fog	Below 50 (below 165)	Disrupts all forms of transport

Fog

Fog is caused by water droplets suspended in the air and sometimes mixed with smoke and dust particles. Fog causes a reduction in visibility in the lower layers of the atmosphere to under 1,000 m (3,300 ft).

Advection fog near Grice Fjord village on Ellesmere Island in the Canadian Arctic. Advection fog is often found in cool sea areas in spring and summer and often affects coastal regions.

TYPES OF FOG

Name	Description
Ice fog	Obscurity is caused by a suspension of minute ice crystals rather than by water droplets
Advection fog	Forms when relatively warm moist air moves over a cool surface
Radiation fog	Forms at night over land when there is a light wind and clear sky. Its formation is very complicated but is involved with how the air cools in a zone around 30 m (100 ft) above the ground and the ground's surface condition
Upslope fog	Develops on the windward slopes of high ground and forms when the air becomes saturated as it is forced to rise by the increasing ground height
Frontal fog	Formed near a weather front when rain falls from warm air into cold stable air below, evaporates and saturates the layer of cold air
Arctic sea smoke	Formed by water evaporating from the surface of cold water and condensing in the cold dry air moving above it; looks like steam rising from the water

Symbols used on weather maps

Meteorologists use the same set of weather symbols so they can more easily compare weather information. Here is a guide to some of them.

FRONTS

Warm front   Cold front   Occluded front

CLOUD COVER

Clear sky	○
1 okta*	◑
2 oktas (¹/₄ cloud cover)	◕
3 oktas	◕
4 oktas (¹/₂ cloud cover)	◐
5 oktas	◑
6 oktas (³/₄ cloud cover)	◕
7 oktas	◑
Overcast (full cloud cover)	●

* An okta represents one eighth of the sky covered by cloud.

WIND SPEED

Calm	◎
1–2 knots	——○
5 knots	⊸○
10 knots	⊸○
15 knots	⊸○
20 knots	⊸○
25 knots	⊸○
30 knots	⊸○
35 knots	⊸○
40 knots	⊸○

SOME INTERNATIONAL WEATHER SYMBOLS

═	☰ ☰	☰
Mist	Patches of shallow fog	Fog
〝	〞	﹐〞
Intermittent slight drizzle	Continuous slight drizzle	Continuous moderate drizzle
●	● ●	❖
Intermittent slight rain	Continuous slight rain	Continuous heavy rain
✳	✳✳	△
Intermittent slight snowflakes	Intermittent moderate snowflakes	Ice pellets
⟨	⟨	
Lightning seen (no thunder heard)	Thunderstorm (no precipitation)	Heavy thunderstorm with rain, snow or sleet
Slight showers of rain	Heavy or moderate showers of rain and snow	Snow pellets or small hail
Moderate or slight sand storm or dust storm	Tornado	Visibility reduced by smoke (e.g. forest fires)

Glossary

acid rain Rain that is more acidic that normal due to the presence of sulphur dioxide and other pollution.

advection fog Fog caused by the condensation of water vapour when warm moist air moves over cold ground or the sea.

air mass A large body of air with a similar temperature and humidity (amount of water vapour).

air pressure The force, or weight, of air on the ground (also called atmospheric pressure).

albedo The amount of light reflected by a surface.

anemometer Instrument used to measure the speed of the wind.

anticyclone A high-pressure weather system, or high, in which the atmospheric pressure is higher than the pressure in the surrounding air. Winds blow around an anticyclone in a clockwise direction in the northern hemisphere and in an anticlockwise direction in the southern hemisphere.

anvil Shape similar to a blacksmith's anvil formed by cirrus clouds at the top of a cumulonimbus when stretched out by high-level winds. Often marks the top of the troposphere.

atmosphere The blanket of gases surrounding the Earth or another planet.

atmospheric pressure see air pressure.

barometer Instrument that measures atmospheric pressure. Falling pressure usually means coming storms. Rising pressure means fine weather.

Beaufort scale Scale used to measure the speed of the wind in a series of numbers from 1 to 12.

blizzard Storm with winds greater than 56 km/h (35 mph) causing major blowing and drifting of snow and severely reducing visibility.

carbon dioxide A gas with no smell or colour given out by animals and absorbed by plants. Too much carbon dioxide gas in the atmosphere results in global warming.

chlorofluorocarbons (CFCs)
Gases made up from chlorine, fluorine and carbon which can damage the ozone layer.

cirrus Wispy white high-altitude clouds made of ice crystals.

cold front The leading edge of a moving body of cold air.

condense To change from a gas or vapour into a liquid or solid.

Coriolis force Name given to the effect of the Earth's spin on winds and ocean currents that follow a curved path across the surface of the Earth. Winds are deflected to the right in the northern hemisphere and to the left in the southern hemisphere.

cumulus Fluffy clouds with cauliflower tops that form in fine weather but may develop into dark storm clouds called cumulonimbus.

cyclone A tropical storm or low-pressure weather system in which winds spiral inwards.

dew point Temperature at which water starts to condense. Dew will form on grass if the temperature falls below the dew point during the night.

downburst Vertical or nearly vertical downwards burst of strong winds near the ground usually associated with a thunderstorm.

dust storm High surface winds with loose dust, reducing visibility to 0.8 km (½ mile).

evaporate To change from a liquid or solid into a gas or vapour.

fossil fuels Coal, oil and natural gas formed from long-dead plants and animals.

front A boundary between different air masses. There are three types of front: warm, cold and occluded. All bring unsettled weather and, usually, rain.

frontal depression A low in which two air masses meet and rotate slowly around a central point bringing unsettled weather.

Fujita–Pearson scale Scale developed by Dr Fujita to classify tornadoes based on wind damage. The scale runs from F0 for the weakest to F5 for the strongest tornado.

glacial Period when large areas of land were covered by ice; also called an ice age.

global warming The warming of the atmosphere due to pollution.

greenhouse effect The warming of the Earth caused by greenhouse gases that allow sunlight to reach the Earth's surface but trap heat given off by the ground.

hemisphere One half of a sphere. The Earth is divided by the equator into the northern hemisphere and the southern hemisphere.

high An area of high atmospheric pressure (see also anticyclone).

humidity The amount of water vapour in the air.

hurricane *see* tropical cyclone.

interglacial Warm period between glacials.

isobar Line on a weather map joining places with the same atmospheric pressure.

jet stream Strong wind in the upper atmosphere that steers storms in the lower atmosphere.

low An area of low atmospheric pressure (see also cyclone).

macroburst Large downburst with damaging winds, up to 4 km (2½ miles) wide.

meteorologist Scientist who studies meteorology, or weather and climate.

microburst Violent downburst less than 4 km (2½ miles) wide.

millibar Unit used to measure atmospheric pressure. The average atmospheric pressure is 1,013 millibars.

monsoon A wind that changes direction according to the season; also the rains it brings to parts of the world during the summer.

mist A reduction in visibility in the lower layers of the atmosphere. The associated visibility is 1,000 m (3,330 ft) or more.

occluded front Front that develops in the later stages of a frontal depression. The term comes from the associated occluding (shutting off) of the warm air at the Earth's surface by a faster-moving cold front.

ozone layer Layer in the atmosphere where the gas ozone is concentrated.

precipitation Deposits of water from the atmosphere that reach the ground as forms of rain, hail and snow.

prevailing wind The most common wind blowing in a particular region.

radiosonde Instrument attached to a weather balloon that transmits air pressure, humidity, temperature, and wind speed and direction as it ascends.

storm surge A rise in the usual water level along the coast as a result of strong winds and/or reduced atmospheric pressure, usually precedes a storm or hurricane.

stratus Low-level grey clouds that form layers. Stratus clouds often produce drizzle.

sunspots Spots that appear on the Sun's surface in 11-year cycles showing extra activity and heat.

temperate Typical warm and mild climate conditions in the middle latitudes.

thunderstorm A storm with thunder and lightning formed in a cumulonimbus cloud, usually with gusty winds, heavy rain and sometimes hail.

tornado Sudden violent storm with a funnel-shaped rotating column of air extending downwards from the base of a cloud.

trade winds Steady easterly blowing winds found on either side of the equator. They blow northeasterly in the northern hemisphere and southeasterly in the southern hemisphere.

tropical cyclone A violent tropical storm with winds blowing at 118 km/h (73 mph) around a centre of low pressure. Also called a hurricane or typhoon.

troposphere The layer of air lying closest to the Earth's surface containing most of our weather.

typhoon *see* tropical cyclone.

visibility The distance you can see owing to the clearness in the atmosphere.

warm front The leading edge of a moving body of warm air.

water vapour Water in the form of an invisible gas.

wind Moving air. Wind direction is the direction from which the wind is blowing.

Index

Note: Page numbers in *italic* refer to captions to illustrations. Main references are in **bold**.

116

Web sites

http://www.meto.govt.uk
The UK Meteorological Office homepage.

http://bbc.co.uk/weather/
For weather reports (local and worldwide) with features and satellite photographs.

EXTREME WEATHER
http://www.meto.govt.uk/sec2/sec2cyclone/tctracks/names.html#NWP2000
For lists of names of tropical storms to be used all over the world from 2000.

http://www.nhc.noaa.gov/
Homepage of National Hurricane Centre (Hurricane Watch) – to find out about and track current hurricanes worldwide.

http://www.fema.gov/kids/hurr.html
Site for kids on what to do if caught in a hurricane; set up by the Federal Emergency Management Agency (FEMA).

http://www.hurricanehunters.com/askus.html
Get answers from the scientists who fly airplanes right into the eye of a hurricane!

http://www.crh.noaa.gov/mkx/owlie/owlie.html
Safety tips on tornadoes, flash floods, lightning, hurricanes, winter weather and carbon monoxide by Owlie, mascot of the National Weather Service and FEMA.

WEATHER CALCULATOR
http://www.srh.noaa.gov.elp/wxcalc/wxcalc.html
Cool tools to help you convert temperature, moisture and pressure readings.

ACTIVITIES AND PHOTOGRAPHS
http://www.whntl9.com/kidwx/index.html
Interactive weather page for kids set up by meteorologists at WHNT TV, Alabama, United States.

http://australiansevereweather.simplenet.com/photography/
Great pictures of clouds, storms, lightning and more.

http://www.goes.noaa.gov/
Real pictures from the geostationary satellite server – take a look at severe weather spots or visit the tropics!

Acknowledgements

l = left; r = right; b = bottom; t = top; c = centre

ILLUSTRATIONS

Alan Collinson Design 63; Richard Bonson 82c; Bill Donahue 83, 86cl; Andrew Farmer 98–99, 100t, 102; Eugene Fleury 27br, 34–35, 49t, 30–31, 53, 72–73 (map and symbols), 85, 95, 110; Mike Foster (Maltings Partnership) 90–91, 92–93; Don Hewitt (The Met. Office College) 111; Gary Hincks 11, 25b, 54–55, 57, 58–59, 61, 62, 66–67, 89; Rob Jakeway 9b, 14, 26, 28–29, 50–51, 86–87b; Mainline Design 12–13b, 75t; Alan Mole 49c; Janos Marffy 18; Jonathan Potter 32; Michael Roffe 66–67 (insets), 72–73 (circular insets); Peter Sarson 3, 79; Peter Sarson/Richard Chasemore 9c, 10, 13r, 16–17, 19, 20, 21, 24, 25b, 25c, 36, 40–41, 43, 44–45, 46–47, 48–49, 51 t, 52, 68, 75b, 77, 84, 94, 100b; Michael Welply 69, 103; Michael Woods 49cr, 82b

PHOTOGRAPHS

4t Digital Vision; 4c The Stock Market; 4b Annie Griffith Belt/Corbis; 5t Popperfoto; 5c Kim Westerskov/ww.osf.uk.com; 5b Andrey Zvoznikov/Planet Earth Pictures; 6/7 Digital Vision; 8 The Stock Market; 9 Digital Vision; 11 Corbis; 12/13 Dennis Flaherty/Planet Earth Pictures, 14, 15, 17 Digital Vision; 19 Kim Blaxland/gettyone Stone; 21, 22, 23, 26/27 The Stock Market; 22/23 NASA/Science Photo Library; 27 Digital Vision; 29 Greg Pease/gettyone Stone; 31 O. Brown, R. Evans and M. Carle, University of Miami Rosenstiel School of Marine and Atmospheric Science; 32/33 Digital Vision; 33 Gavin Smith/Frank Spooner Pictures; 34t,c Digital Vision; 34b Margaret Welby/Planet Earth Pictures; 35tl Digital Vision; 35tc Jean-Marc Dessalas/Frank Spooner Pictures; 35tr, c, br Digital Vision; 35bl Corbis; 37t, c Andrey Zvoznikov/Planet Earth Pictures; 37b Digital Vision; 38/39 Annie Griffith Belt/Corbis; 42 Digital Vision; 43 R. Bird/Frank Lane Picture Agency; 45 JC Allen/Frank Lane Picture Agency; 47 Alan R. Moller/gettyone Stone; 52/53 Steele-Perkins/Magnum Photos, 55 Steve Mccurry/Magnum Photos; 56 Silvia Izquierdo/Popperfoto; 60 Sam Pierson JR/Science Photo Library; 61 Digital Vision; 62/63 Gary Bell/Planet Earth Pictures; 64/65 Popperfoto; 66/67 courtesy of the National Meteorological Library; 66,67 Digital Vision; 68 Steve Mccurry/Magnum Photos; 70 ESA/British Crown copyright; 71t Hank Morgan/Science Photo Library; 71c The Stock Market; 71b NOAA/National Meteorological Library; 72, 73tl, 73b Digital Vision; 73tr John E. Watkins/Frank Lane Picture Agency; 74 Muzzi/Popperfoto; 75, 76, 76/77 Digital Vision; 77 David T. Grewcock/Frank Lane Picture Agency; 80/81 Kim Westerskov/ww.osf.uk.com; 82/83 Bridgeman Art Library; 85 Kim Westerskov/gettyone Stone; 87 Robert M. Carey, NOAA/Science Photo Library; 88 Chris R. Sharp/www.osf.uk.com; 89 George Taylor; 90/91 NASA/Science Photo Library; 91 Laura Wickenden; 95 John Mead/Science Photo Library; 96/97 Andrey Zvornikov/Planet Earth Pictures; 101 Kamal Kishore/Popperfoto; 105 Joe Skipper/Popperfoto; 107 NASA/www.osf.uk.com; 109 E & D Hosking/Frank Lane Picture Agency

COVER PHOTOGRAPHY/ARTWORK

Front l NASA/www.osf.uk.com, r Digital Vision; back Peter Sarson